B E R L I N

AN ARCHITECTURAL HISTORY

▲▌▐ Architectural Design Profile

B E R L I N

AN ARCHITECTURAL HISTORY

GUEST-EDITED BY DOUG CLELLAND

CONTENTS

Editor: Dr Andreas Papadakis

First published in Great Britain in 1983 by *Architectural Design*
AD Publications Ltd, 7 Holland Street, London W8

AD Profile 50 is published as part of Architectural Design Volume 53
11/12 1983

Distributed in the United States of America by St. Martin's Press,
175 Fifth Avenue, New York, New York 10010, USA

ISBN: 0-85670-837-2 (UK)
Library of Congress Catalog Card Number
ISBN: 0-312-07614-2 (USA)

Page 1
Erhart Schön, *Cubic Men*, sixteenth-century engraving.

Frontispiece
Johann Bernhard Schultz, plan of Berlin in 1688, Berlin, Cölln, and Friedrichwerder forming a concentric urban configuration with the Royal Palace in the
centre.

Printed and bound in Great Britain by E.G. Bond Ltd, London

1 Aerial view of Luisenstadt in 1925.

Doug Clelland
Berlin: An Architectural History

2 Krögelgasse nach Norden, Heinrich Zille.

Each moment of fullness bears in itself the negation of centuries of limping and broken history.

André Breton

History probably cannot teach, but it may quietly inspire. Some moments bear fullness while others sterilise and destroy. Breton poses for us the question of assessing 'fullness' and its authentic power to negate what over the centuries can be viewed as empty and worthless.

Such an assessment of the notion of fullness is not a problem of the past as one thing and the present another. Rather our task is to find in the past as in the present those 'moments' when architecture as specific areas of cities or as individual pieces are divested of simplistic ideology and evoke fullness, including fullness of ideas.[2] The value of such moments is consistent, whether we speak of 1680 or 1980.

Assuming therefore that as far as architecture is concerned, there exists an historical dialogue between buildings which evoke fullness from whatever period, the question left relates to the meaning of fullness.

Essentially, fullness in architecture flows from a reflection on the concept of *manifestation*. When architecture as a piece or as an area of a city manifests spatially a set of intentions which inspire or reveal, which declare a negation of limping and broken history be it now or before, and go beyond simplistic ideology, then we can begin to talk of fullness. Manifestation is an act of revelation which renders by the act of building, clearly visible, intelligible and evident fullness of intention.

Today, fullness by way of manifestation cannot as architecture emanate from the primacy of technology, for example, any more than in the early nineteenth century could fullness emanate from the pseudo-mathematics of Durand. To be full is to be complete, mature and rounded, not as expensive irrelevant ornamentation of a basic idea, but as spatial revelation of interacting intentions.[3]

Fullness in an urban area reveals the inspirational qualities of living in a city, while in the individual piece, fullness is that quality which moves architectural space beyond the realm of programme into the realm of imagination and revelation. Such has been known in modern times since Alberti.

Yet, as some would have it, architecture has been assassinated, and any notion of continuity from Alberti merely a scrap of sentimentality and politically reactionary. The assassination of architecture, prompted by the notion that architecture is a dead issue, emanates from a framework of thought which stresses the destructive nature of our modern economies and the destructive cloud which has tinted our heads since the use of nuclear bombs in 1945. The issue today, it is argued, is one of survival, and in such a situation, architecture cannot exist let alone have fullness.

The question, however, cannot be closed at that point. The economic system of mercantilism, which pervaded the eighteenth century, or the religious wars in Europe which were concluded in 1648, for example, both in their own way assassinated architecture. In a profound sense, architecture has always been assassinated or it has not. The history of architecture is neither something to plunder or use; neither therefore the source of historicism nor intelligent cynicism; neither the meaningless pediment nor typological fascination with the likes of the prison, often seen as the ultimate symbol of our age. All this nonsense has always been possible. Rather, the history of architecture may inspire, and as such, it is not assassinated.

What, however, has all this to do with Berlin? For the moment, let us consider Albert Einstein, who lived and worked in Berlin for many years. It is he who more than any, overthrew the Euclidean sense of space which had given order to the fullness of architectural manifestation since its maturity began with classical Greece. It is Einstein who partially inspired the Berlin avant-garde of the early years of our century by introducing into spatial thought a set of propositions very different from the geometry set forth in the *Elements* of Euclid of Alexandria in 300 BC or thereabouts. Now this transformation of the cosmos, and therefore the issue of what analogy of the new cosmos can be built on the surface of the earth as architecture should be a dominant issue today. It is a paradox that at a time when we should be dealing with fragmentation and aesthetic fullness appropriate to our age, most architectural interests appear re-rooted in the soil of Euclidean space, overlaid from time to time with Enlightenment dogmatics. Yet this paradox is somehow inevitable, because Einstein is not Euclid: his work is not so 'perfect'. It is as if today we are living in the equivalent of a pre-Euclidian period, awaiting the clarification of what our cosmos really is and therefore how a horizontal *and* vertical analogue can inspire architecture. As such, our period is caught juggling with two apparently contradictory balls. On the one hand we have a use of history in architectural design which is either cynical, sentimental or fixated by rules. On the other hand we have the understandably American-dominated interest in twentieth-century abstraction and fragmentation.

No theory of architecture can reconcile such interests or clarify our pre-Euclidian mirror. Rather it is in the timeless issues of inspiration and fullness, mediated by the post-Enlightenment abyss which Kleist perceived to be the human condition once the fire of Romanticism had been doused, and which is still the case today, that we can structure our dialogue with our colleagues in history. To amend Breton, each moment of fullness bears in itself the negation of our limping and broken present.

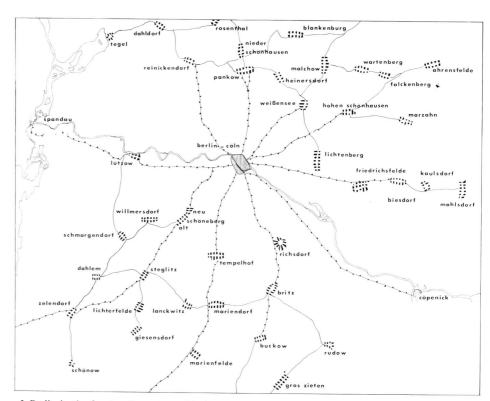

3 Berlin in the fourteenth century with the surrounding villages which were to become absorbed in the growth of the city.

Berlin is not a poetic city in the lyrical sense. As we know, and as will be touched on in this Profile, the city has more than its share of limping and broken history. To describe all that is not my intention here, although it cannot be wished away. Rather its poetry, its ability therefore to offer a penetrative insight into reality, lies in its very hardness. We cannot look to Berlin as we can to Rome to find poetic compositions of ideal forms, but its hardness, an emblem somehow of modernity, has occasioned a long series of inspired moments, in the realms of politics and in the arts and sciences. With the hugely complicated political and architectural process leading up to the Internationale Bauausstellung in 1987, this same conjunction can be found; between the hardness of the location, the interests of a politics which has always been too interested in power, and the attempt somehow to manifest ideal forms as urban architecture. This hardness of place, the constant search for inspiration and the commitment of a population to live the best out of their situation is in a sense the story of Berlin. As far as architecture is concerned, not a wonderful collage of achievement in Berlin, two strands interest me about its history. These strands, one the interest in the *minimal* and the other the interest in the *sensational*, are at work today in the recent transformations in painting and architecture from minimalism to figuration.[4] Berlin is full of the sensational, yet its contribution to the minimal in architecture is definitive, and it is in this latter strand that it may inspire a contemporary understanding of fullness in architecture. As far as the archi-

tecture of the urban area is concerned, Berlin is on a stronger footing. The essential understanding that Berlin offers is the benefit of the block-based structure and configuration over that of more heterogeneous forms, for such a configuration has situated the fragment, has provided the ether, so to speak, in order that the fragments interact and do not simply create inhabited holes in space. For a thing can be a hole. A fragment is only authentic when it implies the whole from which it has been extracted. If, as some believe, the history of Berlin should be taken as a question of excavation, then such a view is only credible if the layers are understood in Breton's terms as moments of fullness rather than empty layers or fragments disassociated from their whole. Fragmentation and wholeness are the twin sides of the same coin. This dialogue is a necessity if contemporary architecture is to be 'full' and explicable.

4 Oranienburger Strasse under construction in 1732. The repetitive nature of the houses is apparent as is the minimalism of the architectural figuration.

In every society one calls by the name of virtue that which is useful to society.
Voltaire

At the close of the religious wars in 1648, Prussia was an extremely poor and insignificant state when compared with her neighbours. Berlin therefore lacked substance as a town. A pragmatic policy of 'toleration' was adopted whereby Protestants and other minorities could settle freely in Prussia, and so long as they paid homage to the State, could be free of religious persecution. The 'degenerate church', as it was called, was replaced by a near contempt for religion; and policies of economic growth and militarism became Prussia's *raison d'être*. None of the major European states wished the expanding power of the Prussians; however, they were to force themselves on to the European stage. In 1706 John Toland, an Englishman who knew Berlin well, wrote enthusiastically about the clarity of vision of the Prussian court in his pamphlet *Christianity not Mysterious*, while Leibnitz, patronised by Sophie Charlotte, became the first President of the Prussian Academy of Sciences after its foundation in 1700. The Academy was based on a rational constitution and Leibnitz' attempts to reconcile science and belief became its main preoccupation. As architecture is determined as built by political and economic power, Prussia in its poverty promoted an architecture which was useful, and while French was the official language, the Berlin of the seventeenth century could only manifest minimal intentions in architecture when compared with the sophisticated and sensational intentions in architecture of Louis XIV's Versailles, and the global ambitions of Colbert. Instead, the more practical and secular cultures of Holland and Flanders influenced the work of architects such as Johann Gregor Memhardt, Michael Mattias Smids and perhaps most important of all, Arnold Nering. The city of the late seventeenth century, held within its fortifications, was centred around the Stadtschloss and its garden, two major churches with their towers and urban squares, and the harbour where the two arms of the Spree met in the south. The early stages of development of Friedrichswerder and Dorotheenstadt, beyond the fortifications, signalled the beginning of the new urban developments which commenced the growth of modern Berlin. Nering, who was responsible for the laying out and construction of the northern part of Friedrichstadt, utilised the army to enforce construction and occupation as the kingdom of Prussia, formed in 1701, wished. He developed techniques of repetitive building and minimal ornamentation on basic house types and represents the tendency to minimalism to be found in Berlin's evolution.

Andreas Schlüter on the other hand had fuller architectural intentions. He arrived in Berlin from Warsaw in 1694 following an extended sojourn in Rome. He settled into a distinguished but traumatic career as Royal Architect. In 1702, he designed a Stadtschloss for Berlin, to be one of approximately twenty

5 South Facade and Principal Plan of the Arsenal by Andreas Schlüter, 1698-1699. Schlüter completed the previous work of Nering and Grünberg.

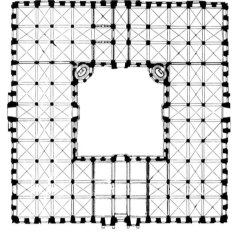

of similar scale in Europe, a project discussed with Fischer von Erlach when the latter was in Berlin in 1704. While Fischer proposed his own Lustschloss, it was Schlüter's proposal which became the basis for what was realised. In 1713, he moved on to St. Petersburg just as most of the fledgling artistic community left Berlin, almost to a man, upon the accession of Friedrich Wilhelm the first, a king who continued the expansion of the minimalist new districts, but who was primarily interested in the economic, social and military growth of Prussia. This iconoclasm, begun in 1713, lasted until 1740, and during this period Prussia became the most disciplined and the most modern military state in Europe.

Returning to Schlüter, he attempted a brave and inspired mission. In a city which lacked a building industry with skills which could be taken for granted elsewhere, Schlüter sought to build an architecture of fullness. Despite the vanguard use of iron in his structures, some of these buildings collapsed because his designs pushed the competence of the industry too far; however, in the many pieces which did not collapse, Schlüter attempted as full an architecture as was possible for a Court which, although economically poor, sought to merge power with an opening of spiritual and intellectual horizons.

The period of the *Aufklärung* (Enlightenment) more or less paralleled the reign of Friedrich the Second (the Great): that is, from about 1740 until 1786. The period can be

characterised in two ways. On the one hand, the military and economic growth of Prussia and Berlin continued, while on the other hand, the intellectual debate, closed down in 1713, was re-opened, with the re-convening of the Academy of Sciences in 1744.

For us, the only way to become great... is by imitation of the ancients.
Winckelmann

In Prussia, the period known in architecture as Neoclassicism began around 1740, although less powerfully in Berlin than elsewhere in the state. While the economic development of Prussia by way of new settlement and urban re-building could be well served by the minimalism inherent in a classicism stripped of Baroque excess, what John Summerson has called 'primitive consideration of structure and utility', the movement was not to gain strength in Berlin until 1786.

Friedrich the Second preferred an architecture closer to the Baroque tradition despite his long association with Voltaire in Berlin, and the intellectual interests of rationalism as set out in his book *The History of My Age*. So while Johann Joachim Winckelmann was to write in 1762, 'Michelangelo started to be licentious and Borromini brought into architecture grand depravity', Berlin continued with its limited resources in the 'old ways'.

6 St Hedwig's Catholic Church by Jean-Laurent Legeay and Boumann. Begun in 1747 and consecrated in 1773, construction was stopped in 1777 and the building was finally completed in 1887.

The concept for Fridericianum, the new cultural centre of Berlin, discloses the architecture approved. It should be seen in the context of a city where nearly one-quarter of the land area was given over to military barracks. In 1746, a Frenchman, Jean-Laurent Legeay, a friend of Piranesi, having spent five years in Rome (where among other studies, he had meticulously surveyed the

7

Pantheon) built the church of St. Hedwig in Berlin. This was the first of the buildings which were to give spatial substance to Friedrich's Forum. The principal architect for these works was Georg Wenzeslaus Von Knobelsdorff whose design for the Opera House was still influenced by themes other than the primitive. The building was dedicated to amateurs of architecture, the drawings annotated in French, with the central internal space conceived as Apollo's chamber. The facades were ornate with classical iconography and sculpture, Apollonian themes being predominant. The pediment encloses the words *Fredericus Rex – Apollini et Muses* and on the whole, the fullness of the intention attempted to address something more than that of arid Prussian pragmatism. The *Mysteries* and the *Muses* were still potent themes for the public architecture of Friedrich's otherwise meticulous Berlin.

7 The Ephraim House in Poststrasse built by Von Dietrichs between 1762 and 1765.

Elsewhere in Prussia, the 'universal will of the state' had different effects on architecture. La Methrie's book *L'Homme Machine* of 1748 was considered by many to be an essential perception of the age, while the growing number of masonic lodges sought 'the intellectual and social unity of man'. Based on the system of 'tolerance' from its own past, Prussia considered social levelling, so crucial to the period in France, unnecessary. In what has been called the 'gambling room' of Europe between 1648 and 1789, Prussia sponsored an architecture of state purpose throughout its territories, and in a wide range of enterprises, more than did any of its greater neighbours. As today, such an architecture tended towards minimalism. The later tradition of functionalism can be easily detected in essence. In the work of David Gilly prior to 1786, for example, we have adequate evidence of this tendency. The 'chilly light of reason', as it has been

8 Jakobshagen (Dobrzany). The top plan illustrates the character of the settlement prior to the work of David Gilly whose proposals are on the bottom plan. Neoclassicism in Prussia began in the provincial areas rather than in Berlin.

described, a dogma formed in Prussia out of the new pragmatic and relatively secular philosophy of toleration, created a morality of efficiency and order. Yet in reality Berlin was a city of imprisoned passions, a city which in 1780, for example, housed more than a hundred brothels, and whose population was losing interest in the failing ambitions of its elites and their *Aufklärung*.

9 The Brandenburg Gate by Carl Gotthard Langhans, 1789–1793.

To see the old world with young eyes makes her young.

Hölderlin

When Friedrich Wilhelm the Second acceded to the throne in 1786, Neoclassicism was finally 'approved', and it cannot be separated from Romanticism. He was a lover of the Arts and open to the new architecture. The building boom in the early years of his reign was supervised by Friedrich Wilhelm von Erdmannsdorf invited to Berlin from Dessau, Carl Gotthard Langhans from Breslau, David Gilly from Stettin and Gottfried Schadow from Rome. The building industry with which they had to work was hardly better than that faced by Schlüter a century before, and Schadow was to write, 'These young architects had to draw every capital, every fillet, doors and floors in full scale for the joiner; because of his tender and noble character, everybody working with him sought to gain his approval.' Erdmannsdorf found it difficult to find collaborators who could draw well. Despite the economic and military achievements of the previous regime, Berlin was still provincial when it came to the quality of the industry which could manifest the intentions of the Neoclassical architects.

The link between Neoclassicism and Romanticism in Berlin is interesting. In the arts and in literature, the move away from what has been called 'arid Rationalism' began about 1773 with the *Sturm und Drang* movement. It is to be noted that Neoclassicism in architecture began to dominate architectural discourse during the 1770s, emanating from Paris, Rome and London. The storm and stresses lying below a surface of efficiency in Prussia needed to be released. While certain images in Berlin portray this, in the work of Chodowiecki for example, one can best recall Goya's crucial work *The Dream of Reason Produces Monsters* of 1797, illustrating the international dimensions of the crisis of the Enlightenment. In Prussia, this period was to end the 'paradise' of compassion and toleration. A deep hostility to French ideas, a need to render Prussia a culture autonomous from that of France, and an interest in Shakespeare and other British cultural achievements were developed. Goethe's life at this time, for example, was an attempted synthesis of classicism, alchemy, the Kabbalah, hermeticism and freemasonry, the latter of which he adopted in 1780. Berlin at this point in its history was perhaps the most tolerant and liberal capital in Europe.

The Romantic inspiration, its attempt to release the human imagination from the now limping and broken history of the *Aufklärung*, addressed the eternal issues of man's being in the world. It was 'the last serious attempt to reconcile subjective consciousness with an ever more puzzling, alien and indifferent universe'.[5] With nature a dominant factor in their sensibility, with its wideness and lack of controlled homogeneity unlike the 'classical' view of nature, the nocturnal and its associations with death become thematically crucial. Where there is death there is life.

10 Monument to Friedrich the Second, Friedrich Gilly, 1797.

This nocturnal view became the fundamental spatial experience of those born around 1770, the mightiest generation that Germany produced since that of Dürer, the generation of Gilly, Friedrich, Runge, Hölderlin, Novalis, Hoffmann, Beethoven, Gorres and the rest.

Sedlmayr

This sensibility, an inspired attempt at making possible fullness in life, but not the resultant abyss of the Romantics, can best be found in the architecture of Friedrich Gilly, who died in 1800 at the age of 28. Before coming to his and his colleagues' work, let us recall aspects of the Romantic inspiration which was all but exhausted as a dominant impulse in Prussia by 1796. They were politically liberal, but not Jacobin and revolutionary. This liberalism, unlike the later German Romantics of post-1815 who were closeted reactionaries, was linked to a primeval sense of eternity and the quasi-religious sense of the eternal. For Steffans, 'A new age is born', while for Friedrich Schlegel, '...I already see the grandest birth of the new age emerging, modest as early Christianity'. The symbols of the 'eye of truth' and the 'tree of liberty' were brought into dialogue with the mysterious and the miraculous. Theatre and life as theatre emerged anew in order that a 'new Republican dawn', as it was called, could emerge; everywhere there was energy seeking moments of fullness. The demise around 1796 can be traced, for example, to their disappointment at developments in France after the 1789 revolution, and their literary organ *The Atheneum* stayed in publication for two years rather than the expected thousand. Yet, 'under Friedrich Wilhelm the Second there emerged in this previously so sober and indeed impecunious and rugged state, a flowering of culture and a wealth of talent which continued for fifty years' (Haffner).

11 The National Theatre of Berlin as proposed by Friedrich Gilly. His competition entry was unsuccessful and the commission went to Langhans.

As my heaven is of iron, so am I myself of stone.

Hölderlin

The latter half of the Romantic impulse and its demise ran parallel to the Neoclassicism of Friedrich Wilhelm's chosen architects. This demise occasioned Heinrich von Kleist to write, 'But paradise is locked and bolted...we have to go on and make the journey round the world to see if it is perhaps open somewhere at the back', but this is inadequate and unhelpful historical material to understand the architectural work centring on Friedrich Gilly, Heinrich Genz and the young Karl Friedrich Schinkel. While intellectual life was limping and broken around them, they achieved a manifestation of architectural ideas of great fullness.

13 The Vieweg Publishing House Building.

Genz and Gilly, working a full generation after Ledoux and Boullée, founded the 'Association of Young Architects' who came together in Berlin in order to work on the solution to ideal architectural problems. They did not attempt to supplant the older and less inspired official architects, but rather sought the development of their work through drawing and teaching. It can be validly observed that a minimalism influenced their thinking, but not merely for academic purity; indeed, their interpretations of classical buildings, despite the availability of the standard archeological and architectural treatises, are often confused. The minimal was of interest because the eternal and cosmic of the Romantics and the genuine three-dimensional sensuality of perception gained from the Baroque were sufficiently full not to require ornament. Gilly's sketches for a Pfeilerhalle, for example, probably a mausoleum for freemasons, is stripped of all ornament and has a plan determined in all likelihood by the summer and winter solstices. The sensational for these architects, and the fragmentary nature of figuration, was not decadence, but a workable set of architectural intentions which sought to reveal dimensions of human life higher than those of pragmatic reality.

14 The Mint, Berlin by Heinrich Genz, 1798.

Erdmannsdorf was to write: 'These drawings [buildings of classical Rome] should not give the student unchangeable fixed rules (like the column canons of the French Academics); he should learn to see the building parts in relation to each other and to the whole; he should not subject art to measured regulations and should not degrade it to a mechanical business.'

12 The Vieweg Publishing House Building in Braunschweig by David Gilly, 1800–1805. Burgplatz before and after construction of the building.

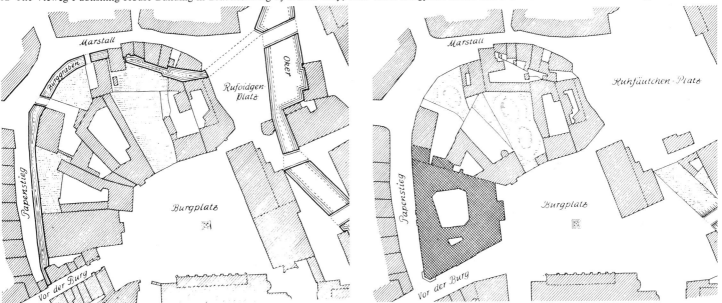

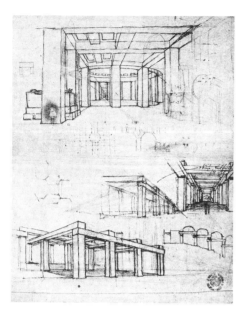

15 The Pfeilerhalle project by Friedrich Gilly, 1796.

16 Proposal for a Stair Hall by Schinkel, 1803.

17 Ehemaliges Steinmeyersches Haus in Friedrichstrasse by Schinkel, 1803.

Genz responded to critics of his Mint building thus: 'The architectural composition is based on the character of this building which is one of the first and most important factories in the country'.

Friedrich Becherer, a student and collaborator of Gontard, conducted the architectural class at the Academy, and when it became the more autonomous Bauakademie, Friedrich Gilly, a professor of Optics and Perspective, was to become one of the most influential teachers of his day. His exhibited projects also inspired, and it was by seeing Gilly's *Monument to Frederick the Great* that Schinkel decided to take up architecture. Levetzow, speaking of this project, reports from a conversation with Gilly in 1796: 'We agreed fairly soon, that merely a statue was not enough, but that an architectural work would be appropriate, which should serve as a national sanctuary combining all the grandeur and majesty which could be achieved by way of this project. At the same time the monument should be a vehicle of great moral and patriotic purpose, as it was the case with the large public buildings and monuments of the Old.'

'The temple should be erected on the Leipziger Platz on top of a rectangular base... In the interior of which Friedrich's sarcophagus, his library and a museum Fridericianum should be housed.

Napoleon entered Berlin through the Brandenburg Gate in 1806 appearing among cheers as the embodiment of the Caesarian hero. One recalls Bonaparte's campaign in Egypt in the years 1798 to 1799, when Denon, Napoleon's war correspondent wrote in *Voyage dans la Haute et Basse Egypte* about the first sighting of the ancient ruins of Thebes, 'The army arrived in the evening on the heights; the soldiers were struck dumb with amazement; they then broke into loud

acclamation. They voluntarily helped the archeologists working there'.

The Antique, the Romantic sensibility, the Hero and a political tendency towards liberal democracy conjoined to address Breton's challenge to fullness. With the young Schinkel we find the last remnants of this form of inspiration in Berlin.

How are the mighty fallen.
                                    Byron

In the Vienna Congress during the years 1814-1815, Europe was politically reconstructed on the basis of eighteenth-century power patterns. The restoration of pre-revolutionary structures of authority were implemented under the direction of Metternich. The second generation of German Romantics, motivated by similar themes as their predecessors became as politically reactionary as their political peers. This 'return to order', as it was called, was welded to the efficient and bureaucratic tradition of Prussia and Berlin, and created the conditions under which Karl Friedrich Schinkel worked until his death in 1841. 'While Heine and Gorres were on the run from the Prussian censor – indeed from Prussian warrants for arrest – Schinkel and Rauch were beautifying Berlin and Mendelssohn discussed the St. Matthew Passion. Academic life in Beidermeier Prussia also had a dual face. Never had the University of Berlin listed more brilliant names: Hegel and Schelling, Savigny and Ranke; yet at the same time, hundreds of rebellious students disappeared behind prison walls' (Haffner).

Schinkel's professionalism is a remarkable achievement, and aspects of his work are discussed by Julius Posener later in this Profile. While in Berlin today we can still see many of his buildings, we can hardly gain an impression of the city he transformed, not by way of grand planning schemes, but by way of piecemeal autonomous insertions which show a

dexterity not often apparent in the autonomous architecture of our own century. Rather his work, despite the social bankruptcy of his society, emanated from the reality of partial fulfilment of ideal aims. Not altogether content with this, however, Schinkel embodied his interest in grand planning either in the reconstruction of antique villas or in proposals for the capital cities of other nations.

18 Plan for Athens by Schaubert, Kleanthes and Schinkel.

Goethe had said of Berlin, 'My whole heart yearned to quit this city of splendid misery and miserable splendour,' while he had called Berliners 'a dare-devil race'. With a strong political order under which to work, Schinkel, called 'a prince' by Friedrich Wilhelm the Third, set about improving the public image of Berlin. On his death in 1841, the city was still relatively small, having a population of some 400,000 inhabitants. The social revolution of 1848, which failed, confirmed Hegel's view about the French revolution that, 'Once the realm of imagination has been revolutionised, reality will not stand up'. Schinkel's achievement belongs to the old period of a small Berlin and a relatively powerful Prussia. It is often an over-estimated era from which only professional inspiration can be drawn.

Railways, express mails, steamboats, and all possible means of communication are what the educated world seeks.
                                    Goethe

In the moment in which architects start making use of the new materials which industry has made available, a new architecture will have come into being.
                           Boetticher (1846)

19 James Hobrecht, Development Plan for Berlin and its surroundings, 1862.

20 Typical block and street plan of *Mietskasernen'*.

The period from 1850 to 1914 witnessed the dawn of Modernism in Berlin which was to explode with enormous energy in the 1920s. In architecture, the period after Schinkel has no singular achievements comparable to his. It is nevertheless an era of grand propositions and huge and painful confusions. To give an impression of the metropolitan labyrinth that Berlin was to become in a short text like this is not worth undertaking. What I shall do is to offer a longish quotation from James Hobrecht, chief of building control in Berlin, who in 1862 espoused the reasons why the rapidly growing city was to be developed as a street and layered urban block form of configuration, rather than the more heterogeneous form favoured in England at the same time and typified by London. While reading the following excerpt from his essay *Concerning Public Health*, it is important to bear in mind the fact that Berlin *did* have under its influence sufficient land suitable for

a more decentralised policy. 'It is known that our way of life stands on an opposite principle to that of the English way of living. In the so-called *Mietshaus*(apartment building) there is on the first floor a flat for a rent of 500 taler; on the ground floor and on the second floor there are two flats each for 200 taler; on the third floor there are two flats each for 150 taler; on the fourth, three flats each costing 100 taler; in the cellar, the garret, the rear courtyard building, or in other similar spaces, there are several other flats rented for 50 taler. In English towns, situated close together, there are villas and single houses of the wealthy classes to be found in the western areas and elsewhere, while in the other districts of the town, the houses of the poorer population are to be found, put together in groups according to the fortunes of the owners; complete districts of cities are inhabited by the working population. Who wants to doubt that the reserved areas of the wealthy classes and their houses offer enough comfort, but who can close his eyes to the fact that the poorer classes lose many benefits. Not "seclusion" but "integration" seems to me requisite for ethical and therefore political reasons. In the *Mietskaserne* (rental barracks), the children living in the basement flats, go through the same entrance-hall to the *Freischule* (elementary school free of charge) as do those of the councillor or merchant on their way to the *Gymnasium* (grammar school). Wilhelm Schuster from the attic and the old bedridden Mrs Schulz in the backhouse, whose daughter earns their scanty living by sewing and cleaning, become people known to those living on the first floor. Here is a bowl of soup for strengthening a sick person, there a garment, some efficient help to gain free tuition or something similar – and all this is the result of the comfortable relationships between inhabitants of the same kind, even if their living standards are so different – a help which has an ennobling influence on the donor. And between these extreme social classes, the poorer people of the third and fourth floor move about among social classes which are of the highest significance for our cultural life, the official or public servant, the artist, the scholar, the teacher and so on. These classes embody above all the spiritual and intellectual significance of our people and nation. Forced to constant work, to frequent renunciation, while forcing themselves not to lose their position in society for which they had to struggle, even to raise it if possible, they are by their example and teaching, elements in Society which cannot be esteemed highly enough. As they promote and stimulate, they are useful to society, even if it is only their being and their mute example which has an effect on those who live besides and among them.
An English working-class district is entered only by the policeman and the writer seeking sensation. If a young English lady were to read his alarming novel, she would probably burst into tears, order the carriage, and go into the districts never entered by her kind

before, a destination to which the coachman, shaking his head, would have difficulty in finding the way. As a rule, this bath would be too strong for her nerves; she shudders at the poverty, she shudders at the evil and the crime seen everywhere as a companion of poverty which is left to its fate. She returns home in order not to witness this horrible area again and she salves her soul by paying money destined for a pauper-commission.[7]

21 The Mendelssohm Bank, Jagerstrasse 52, by Martin Gropius built between 1872 and 1873.

This 'integrated' form of urban development was to be largely the norm until after 1945 and the programmes of reconstruction which followed on from the Second World War. Such urban areas are still to be experienced today in Charlottenburg and Kreutzberg in West Berlin and in Prenzlauerberg in East Berlin.

22 'Dampfmaschinenhaus' in Potsdam by Ludwig Persius built between 1841 and 1843. Persius took over a number of projects from Schinkel when the latter died in 1841.

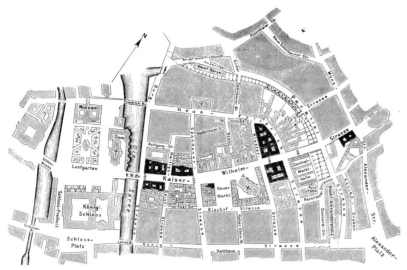

23 Blocks designated for demolition and improvement in the old sector of Berlin, 1877 to 1884.

24 The Erechtheion Hall of the New Museum built by Stüler between 1843 and 1859.

Such formation of a city came as we know with enormous social evils and was prime propaganda for the 'knock it all down' brigades in the 1920s, 1950s and 1960s, although it has been said of Berlin: 'Slums were less prevalent in Prussia than in England owing to the comparatively recent development of most industrial cities, but during the 1890s, living conditions in the working class districts of German cities deteriorated with the influx of newcomers; there were no uniform standards and over-crowding tended to increase'.[8]

Nevertheless, it is all too easy to assess the Berlin of the second half of the nineteenth century simply in terms of what were the human effects of what are called 'rental barracks (*Mietskasernen*)' where the living conditions *were* appalling. This assessment, which has been predominant, chooses to ignore the fact that most *Mietshäuser*, the blocks which contained them, and the network of streets, provided a more than

acceptable urbanity for the majority of the population. Walking in Charlottenburg today, or living in a flat in such an area, easily confirms that such urban form can inspire a search for the ways of spatially providing for quality of living in a city.

After Prussia's armies dominated France in 1870, and Berlin became the capital of a unified Germany, we enter a period known as the *Grunderjahre*, when decadent sensationalism and little minimalism informed the architecture of the city. Yet as with all great cities, opinions should be divided.

One observer [Karl Scheffler – art critic] complained that it seemed to be Berlin's fate to be 'always becoming and never being'. The streets were constantly torn up and rebuilt; familiar landmarks disappeared and were replaced by architectural horrors chosen by the nouveaux riches. Berlin itself seemed to be a parvenu when compared with the settled beauty of

Paris and Vienna, or the grandeur of Rome and London.

Gerald Masur

The Berlin Renaissance was a process that began fifteen years before the First World War. When I got there in 1908 it was already a golden age. It was a coming together of the best brains and the most creative artists in Europe.

Edgar Varèse

The German Chicago – it is a new city, the newest I have ever seen. Chicago would seem venerable beside it... the next feature that strikes one is the spaciousness, the roominess of the city. There is no other city, in any country, whose streets are so generally wide... only parts of Chicago are stately and beautiful, whereas all of Berlin is stately and substantial, and it is not merely in parts, but uniformly beautiful.

Mark Twain

25 Plan for Athens, Ludwig Hoffman.

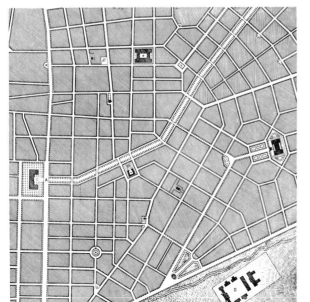

26 Café Bauer in Unter den Linden in 1900. This was the first Viennese café in Berlin.

Modernism and suburbanisation begin to edge into prominence. The former is essentially urban while the latter becomes the stuff of architecture. Architecture begins to slide into its uninspired state, and Muthesius, who claimed that '...apartment house living was a poor substitute for the one family house', exemplifies the tasteful oblivion into which residential architecture has disappeared until recent years in continental Europe – and indeed in Berlin.

Ludwig Hoffmann, city architect from 1886 until 1924, is not an inspired architect. Nevertheless, he builds *for* the city and therefore, despite his classicism, is in sympathy with the urban roots of Modernism.

With respect to architecture as the piece, the period after Schinkel is not inspired. Accepting, however, that architecture was dwarfed by the sensationalism of the time and the phenomenon of the Metropolis, we may find that these very facts lead us to a knowledge of essential aspects of urbanity; a knowledge by means of which the merits of intensity in urban life can be separated from the unacceptable features of density.

The post-1815 power structure in Berlin brought Prussian leadership to a united Germany. It created the conditions for the burgeoning metropolis, and due to the politically reactionary leadership, it prevented widespread participation in the shaping of that metropolis. Due to this, urban densities of population ensued in *some* districts, which resulted in gross over-occupation of the urban blocks. Architecturally, no clear representation of the period is discernible, nor was the manifestation of fullness apparent in those buildings which were free of the economic and speculative strictures of state or private demands. However, the representation of a vital urban culture was achieved. By the adoption of the *Mietshaus* and *Wohnhaus* forms, the internal courtyards, the urban block and the street; by the fact

that these primary urban forms were capable of variation; by the encouragement of multiplicity of occupation in most buildings (the street level invariably being used for non-residential dwelling); and by the fact that an intense atmosphere and sociability ensued as a public realm, while most flats were large enough for civilised family life, the Berlin of the nineteenth century, apparent in so many 1920s films such as Ruttman's *Symfonie der Grosstadt* of 1927, contributes to an appreciation of urbanity as a desirable human condition.

This urban labyrinth played host to the rise of Modernism.

With writers endlessly issuing manifestoes, founding movements, forming coteries, establishing theatre groups, publishing periodicals, pronouncing, protesting, declaring, associating and dissociating and again reassociating, politicking, polemicizing, manoeuvering, enthusing and abusing, the city had generated an intense cultural excitement.

James McFarlane

Without a Crystal Palace, life is a burden.
Bruno Taut

The end of the First World War appeared to many to be the commencement of a new age, to be inhabited by new people living in a new city made up by a new architecture. The Jansen Plan, which won the 1910 'Gross Berlin' competition, was viewed as limping reformism unsuitable to the new international solidarity against the history which had given rise to the atrocities of the war. 'In February 1917, the surrealist painter Max Ernst and I were at the front, hardly a mile away from each other. The German gunner, Max Ernst, was bombarding the trenches where I, a French infantryman, was on the lookout. Three years later, we were the best of friends, and ever since, we have fought

fiercely side by side for one and the same cause, that of the total emancipation of man' (Paul Éluard).

From one battle to the next. In fact, the metropolis of Berlin, as constructed in the eighteenth and nineteenth centuries, survived intact the radical architecture of the 1920s, the politically reactionary and Neoclassical tendencies of the same decade, and the 1930s plans of Hitler and Albert Speer.

The 1920s were essentially pluralistic and a reading of the journal *Deutsche Bauzeitung*, a middle ground architectural publication, establishes this fact without doubt, as does the recently re-published 27,000 pages of *Die Weltbuhne,* the key organ of critical thought throughout the period. This pluralism in the post-war period is best exemplified by two built projects. 1926 a year often associated with the dominance of the 'new architecture', witnessed the construction of the new City Museum in Düsseldorf by Wilhelm Kreis. This building is in strict Neoclassical garb. On the other hand, the 1930s, a period normally associated with Nazi Classicism, saw the building of Koller's Volkswagen estate in Wolfsburg in strictly *Neues Bauen* form. These two examples characterise the architectural polarities of the post-war period.

During the years immediately after the war, a spiritually motivated and utopian architecture evolved in Berlin. With the knowledge that the city required between 100,000 and 130,000 new apartments in order to ease the overcrowding and to house the burgeoning population, the *Arbeitsrat für Kunst* (Working Council for Art), the nucleus of the 'Novembergruppe', was established in November 1918. Its ambition, the 'unification of the arts under the wing of a great architecture', was initially sensationalist and visionary, and one of its key members, Walter Gropius, praised the power of imagination over that of technology. The work of the time accentuates colour and openness, not a feature of Berlin as a city, yet the work has another, more sinister, dimension. The heritage of the war occasioned Gropius to say: 'A breach has been made with the past, which allows us to envisage a new aspect of architecture corresponding to the technical civilisation of the age we live in; the morphology of dead styles has been destroyed; and we are returning to honesty of thought and feeling'.

The 'dead' buildings of Berlin's architectural history are to absorb those of Alberti, Palladio, Borromini *et al*, while the 'street canyons' of the city are to be replaced by the canons of 'Air, Sun and Light'. Such ambitions, on the one hand the search for a quasi-religious spirituality, and on the other hand a stance to completely reject the past are to be achieved by what was called 'Total Design'. In Luçkhardt's *Monument to Work*, for example, the colours are new, but the hordes of people at the base of the tower are as helplessly passive and manipulated as at any time in the would-be detestable history of architecture. Some years later, in his

27 Wassily Luckhardt, *Monument to Work*, 1917.

project for a 'Total Theatre' for Piscator, Gropius sought the 'mobilisation of all three-dimensional means to shake off the audience's intellectually directed apathy, to overwhelm them, to stun them, and *to force them*[9] to participate in experiencing the play.' The totalitarian dimension to the architectural production after the war discloses an emphasis of which we are becoming more aware.

The proletarians did not care for the proletarian theatre – it died without mourning in April of 1921.
Frau Piscator

The spiritual outburst lasts until 1924. In that year, after crippling inflation in Germany and the optimistic years of revolution in Russia, policies became more pragmatic, a significant amount of building was achieved, and the spiritual outburst was replaced by practical thought. As far as Berlin is concerned, this would continue unabated until 1929 and in a lesser way until 1933 and the coming to power of Hitler. The role of Martin Wagner, who replaced Ludwig Hoffmann as City Architect in 1924, the latter retiring not because of lack of political support, but because of regulations on the retirement age of civil servants, is considered in detail later in this Profile.

In 1930, Mies van der Rohe, who was director of the Bauhaus, impatient with demands for democracy from left-wing students said, 'You are here to work and learn. Anyone not present in his classes in the morning will be expelled.' Clearly tensions were ripping apart even the progressive institutions of the *Neue Sachlichkeit* (New Objectivity), just as had happened within the progressive institutions of the *Aufklärung*. The problems with this form of progress have long been debated, and '...this quite necessary and inevitable step forward will be a reactionary affair – *Neue Sachlichkeit* is reactionary'. (Berthold Brecht).

With no clear concensus among the left on politics and architecture, the way was open for the onslaught of the Nazis:

The new dwelling is an instrument for the destruction of the family and the race.
Paul Schultze-Naumberg

The Nazi reality, with its beginnings in 1920 as the 'German Workers Party' are upon us. Before touching on the limping and broken history, absent of any moments of fullness, which is to be the lot of Berlin until 1945, let us recall some aspects of the Weimar Republic which touch on architecture.

I seek, 'the dwelling for the subsistence level'.
Ernst May

The new style thus came to be considered by many of Germany's most influential critics as primarily a set of solutions to the technical and sociological questions.
Barbera Miller-Lane

28 Ludwig Hilberseimer, *Business District in a Metropolis*, 1924.

Grosz thus points an early warning finger towards the totalitarianism not only of Speer and Troost, but of Bruno Taut, Ludwig Hilberseimer, Hannes Meyer and the arch-megalomaniacal mechanic himself Le Corbusier.
Calvorcoressi

Hitler is not Mussolini. Berlin will never be capital of a Fascist Reich. Berlin remains red.
Vorwärts (1933)

Constructivism is the socialism of vision.
Laszlo Moholy-Nagy

I enjoy decadence, and I also enjoy democracy. Berlin then was about as decadent as it is humanly possible to be, but it was also fairly democratic. It even seemed to be moving towards socialism, and that would have been ideal – socialism and self-gratification at the same time.
Kenneth Tynan

And so we were against all ideology, because the ideology based on Kant and Fichte and Hegel had become compatible with war. We were against culture because the culture of Goethe and Schiller had become compatible with war.
Richard Huelsenbeck

29 Peter Behrens, High Tension Power Plant for AEG, 1910. The classicism which was to return in Behrens' project for AEG on Speer's north-south axis is apparent.

And there was an immense range of things going on, though we Berliners had little idea, at the time, how far reaching, how long lasting these trends and developments were to be.
Egon Larsen

When I hear the word culture, I reach for a gun.
Herman Goering

I hate Berlin... a monster city of stone and asphalt.
Joseph Goebbels

Berlin is a big city, but not a true metropolis... we must surpass Paris and Vienna.
Adolf Hitler

We approach the end of the period covered in this Profile. The tendency to Classicism in the 1920s became clearly associated with a totalitarian regime. The Wall Street crash of 1929 brought in a new economic age, with Britain coming off the Gold Standard, the first of the five-year economic plans being devised in the Soviet Union, and the New Deal being introduced in America. By 1940, a new economic order was in place, and the National Socialist revolution in Germany (a nation more seriously affected by the final economic breakdown of the old economic order in the 1920s than most), was part of profound changes in world affairs. The Nazi regime and its architecture, however, must be seen for what they were – one of the most barbaric challenges to human reason, dignity and values ever witnessed.

Around us a new Germany must rise, which can find a home in dwellings embedded in foliage, whose government buildings no longer look like factories, nor its churches like movie houses, but instead bear the signature of the majesty and the power of the people.
Paul Schulze Naumberg

30 Albert Speer, north-south axis, Berlin. The relationship between urban space studied in detail and military formations. The lowest point in the human ebb from which moments of fullness can be built up.

The Nazis attempted to create a world empire which unlike earlier examples was not 'accompanied by an opening of spiritual and intellectual horizons which raised humanity to a new level of consciousness'.[10] It was argued that 'Old Europe' had been centred on London. The new 'freer organism' of international order, as it was called, was to be centred on Berlin. The city was to have a population of ten million inhabitants, was to be completed with the spoils of an easy war by 1950 and was to be called 'Germania'. The responsibility for the design of central Berlin fell to Albert Speer. Only 40 years of age when the Soviet Union finally overran the city in 1945, he had established a team of young architects who, under his brilliant management, had received private commissions of huge proportions, all designed in the monumental classical style favoured by the regime. Speer's 'Master Plan' was backed by unprecedented legal powers. Not only had he control over the design of all buildings of all types, but he also had the financial means to expropriate any land required. Although Speer possessed this power, the dream of the most ardent reformers of the 1920s and the 1950s, and today still the dream of the same creed albeit often in classical costumes, the war effort and result, thankfully prevented its use.

This period of architectural history is currently being exposed to the rigours of research, as part of the fascination or exorcism of Nazism now popular among German intellectuals. But, as with architectural style, such plans and ambitions cannot be separated from the many thousands of specific events of horrible cruelty, and the cynical view of mankind which went to bend the German peoples' minds and to make up what has now entered consciousness as the Holocaust.

Despite a promise to Speer that he would leave Berlin before it was destroyed completely, Hitler changed his mind, and on his order of March 19th 1945, 'Germany was to be made one vast wasteland. Nothing was to be left with which the German people might somehow survive their defeat'.[11] This somehow is an apt point to offer some concluding remarks, for it is the lowest point of the human ebb, and as we are aware a great deal of building up has occurred during the past 38 years.[12] Before this building up began, not only architecture, but any reasonable human behaviour was threatened with assassination.

I have perhaps spent more time on 'limping and broken history' than I had intended at the outset; nevertheless this is required if the true power of the meaning of 'moments of fullness' is to be grasped. Berlin and Prussia *are* modern phenemona. As such they inform us on what *is*, rather on the myths of what ought to be or what could be. Our modernity has been dominated by secularisation and the primacy of economics even though the strands of deeper culture are with us more than many would allow. The era covered can only be viewed relatively, and this too is of our age; the cycles of similar interests are found at some times in the hands of those who seek imagination and emancipation and at other times in the hands of those who seek otherwise. As throughout the modernity of Berlin, so now. In this sense, history cannot teach. Too much, especially ideology, is relative.

As to the notion of human emancipation which has appeared in various forms throughout the period covered, Jung has said, 'I have come across dreams of modern people that have to do with Berlin. In these dreams Berlin stands as a symbol of the psychic weak spot – the place of danger – and for this reason is the place where the self is apt to appear.' Modernity *is* a place of danger and with all its relativities, it is the appearance of self that holds the key to the question of survival and therefore to the question of the state of architecture: whether assassinated or not.

Do what he will, [man] is an inheritor.
                                    Sedlmayr

Berlin as a modern phenemona poses for us the meaning of inheritance. Breton's choice is apt – either to inherit all the problems and complexes of 'limping and broken' history, or to inherit 'each moment of fullness' as a means of dealing with what is. With respect to architecture, this is a matter of intellectual courage and compositional fullness. As such we can choose from the history of any city those who we can call colleagues.

The principle of freedom is unimpugnable and irrevocable. It is no longer possible for anyone still to affirm the unfreedom of humanity. The principle that all are free never again can be shaken.[13]

The philosophy is clear, let the architecture follow.

Notes
1. This introduction condenses 50 pages of manuscript originally prepared for this Profile. Four essays 'Berlin in the years 1688–1848 – Architecture in the Turmoil of Prussian Secular Culture'; City without Architects –Berlin as Labyrinth and Metropolis'; 'Berlin in the Weimar Republic – The Continuity of the Metropolis and the Impotence of Conflicting Ideologies'; and 'Germania –From Metropolis to Wasteland – Berlin in the years 1933 to 1945', have given way for reasons of space.
2. Ideology is 'the science of ideas; that department of philosophy or psychology which deals with the origin and nature of ideas' (OED).
3. These terms 'fullness' and 'revelation' are consistent with reason as people are still moved by the concreteness of beauty and the extended world in a piece of architecture which goes further than the rational and the pragmatic.
4. For a discussion of this point as far as painting is concerned, the reader is referred to the essay, 'Flesh and the Devil in Figure Painting' by Marjorie Welish, in *Partisan Review*, no.4, 1983.
5. *An Abyss Deep Enough – Letters of Heinrich von Kleist*, from the Introduction by Philip B. Miller, page 6.
6. *Die Bauwerke und Kunstdenkmäler von Berlin* by Hermann Schmitz.
7. *Das Steinerne Berlin*, Werner Hegemann, 1930, pages 232–233.
8. 'The Urbanising World' by Eric E. Lampard in *The Victorian City – Images and Realities*, Volume 1, Edited by Dyos and Wolff, page 24.
9. Italics added.
10. 'World Empire and the Unity of Mankind' by Eric Voegelin, in *World Technology and Human Destiny*, page 171.
11. *The Rise and Fall of the Third Reich* by William L. Shirer, page 1311.
12. See for example *Architectural Design*, 52 11/12 – 1982, 'Post-War Berlin'.
13. *Reason in the Age of Science* by Hans-Georg Gadamer, page 37.

31 Friedrich Gilly, sketch of the route, May 1797.

Acknowledgements
I would like to thank 19, 29, and 39 for all the help they have given me on this Profile over the years, and to the many in Berlin and London with whom the subject has been discussed.

Ernst Badstübner
Berlin – Its History and Face from the Thirteenth to the Seventeenth Century

Origins and Establishment

Berlin is a young city. When the major German cities had already reached the peak of their architectural development (not only in the west where core settlements went back to Roman times, but on the eastern border as well), Berlin had not yet been established. At the end of the twelfth century, new rings of walls were built around Cologne on the Rhine and Magdeburg on the Elbe, enclosing the older ports, the fringe areas and planned extensions; this determined the city areas for a long time to come, far beyond the Middle Ages. These cities were by then fully-fledged legal institutions; their social structure was becoming more differentiated and classes were becoming more distinct in terms of occupation and property. Where Berlin was to grow there was at this time only a small settlement of German merchants, presumably colonists, but even they had not been on the site for long. At least another two generations were to pass before a community had grown up which could be given the legal status of a town. But after that, the development came quickly and by the end of the thirteenth century the ground plan had been created which Berlin was to retain until the middle of the seventeenth century. The map drawn by Johann Gregor Memhardt and published in Merian's *Topographia* in 1652 still shows the city as it was built in the thirteenth century.

Whether the original choice of site for the settlement was for trade and transport or strategic considerations has recently come under dispute.[1] The high plateau of Teltow and Barnim stretching far into the Spree valley and the sand-banks between the branches of the rivers created favourable land routes, offering a good site for a trading place with a castle-like fortification for its protection. Known as the 'Alter Hof' (Old Court), this is believed to be the precursor of the Margrave's court. It is thought to have stood first to the south of the ford and later on the eastern edge of the city, where eventually the

1 Ground plan of the two residence towns of the Kurfürst Berlin and Cölln on the Spree by Johann Gregor Memhardt from 1652.

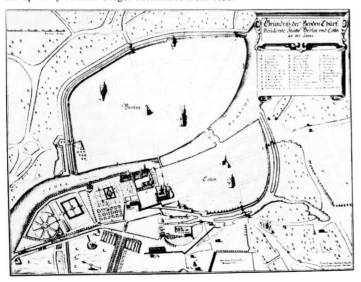

'Hohes Haus' (High House), the seat of the territorial ruler and his offices, was to stand in Klosterstrasse, before the 'Residenz' was built on the island in the Spree.[2]

The assumption that a fortress erected by the territorial ruler formed the beginning of Berlin remains a hypothesis. However, it is certain from the discovery of several graves under the foundations of the Church of St. Nicolas, the first monumental building in Berlin, that a settlement existed before the town was laid out to a specific plan. As these were Christian burials, the settlers were probably Germans who had penetrated this far, following the Ascanian conquest of the Slavic territories around the Elbe River to the west. They had laid the basis for a trading post, taking advantage of the route through the Spree valley.[3] This cannot have been before the last decades of the twelfth century, and at this time the settlement must have been the most advanced eastern outpost of the German colonists under the leadership of the Ascanians. Certainly this would justify a protective military structure.

Around 1140 the Ascanians, nobility from the Harz Mountains in central Germany, began under Albert the Bear the second conquest of the Slavic territory to the east of the Elbe around the Havel and the Spree; the ultimate aim was the Oder and the route to the Baltic. In 1157 they had acquired the former power centre of the Hevellers or Stodorans in Brandenburg.[4] After 1170 they are assumed to have been in western Teltow and to have reached the line roughly from the Templar settlement of Tempelhof through Mariendorf to Marienfelde (south of present-day Berlin). At the same time, the old Slavic fortress of Spandau on the conjunction of the Havel and the Spree, a major strategic point for further expansion, was taken by the Ascanians — a warden is mentioned for the first time in 1197 — and it was probably around this time that the narrow pass in the Spree valley, which until then had not been populated even by the Slavs, was occupied.

But further to the east in the Spree territory, in eastern Teltow and in Barnim, the supremacy of the Slavic princes who resided in Köpenick was not yet broken, and the Margraves of Meissen from the House of Wettin, rivals from the south to the Ascanians in the drive eastwards, opposed a further advance to the middle Oder (Lebus). So the Ascanians first moved north up the Havel, skirting Barnim as far as the lower Oder (Oderberg, Schwedt). As long as the high plateaux were not taken, the position of the settlement between them on the Spree remained insecure. But then, and this cannot have been before the second decade of the thirteenth century, the ford acquired a greater importance. This was to increase further when the Ascanians gained control of the situation on the upper reaches of the Spree between 1225/30 and 1240. It is hardly likely that the territorial rulers initiated the building of the city to a specific plan before that date. For lack of more specific information there is thus no reason to doubt the date 'around 1230' given in older research on Berlin as the date of foundation. We can include Berlin, as has always been the case, among those cities which received their civic rights from the joint rulers Johann I (1225-66) and Otto III (1225-67).[5]

Position and Expansion

Berlin is first mentioned in documents in 1244, and its sister city Cölln on the Spree island (the foundation of dual cities on a river crossing was quite frequent) is mentioned in 1237. In each case a certain Symeon is mentioned, the first time as 'Plebanus', the second as 'Praepositus'; such appellations presuppose church institutions, and we can point to the parish churches of St. Peter in Cölln and St. Nicolas in Berlin. In the regular rectangular street network of the two cities on the Memhardt map the quarter around St. Nicolas stands out, with blocks of houses separated by streets radiating out from the church. This phenomenon is to be found in several cities founded in the Mark Brandenburg (region) in the thirteenth century, and E. Jobst Siedler has described it as the 'core settlement'[6], consisting of a market and a church dedicated to St. Nicolas (patron saint of sailors and travelling merchants) and forming the basis for the planned layout after establishment. The market in the Berlin core settlement was formed from the fork in the routes across the river, one leading downstream to Spandau and one upstream to Stralau. To this day these streets retain the old three-cornered ground plan known as the Molkenmarkt. The streets which ran parallel to the river after the fork, Spandauerstrasse and Stralauerstrasse, became the backbone of the street network. The oblique angle at which they meet at the Molkenmarkt causes the parallel streets and the surrounding wall to bend in that part of the city laid out first (the south-east). So the curving streets are not a result of the junction with the radial arrangement around the Church of St. Nicolas, as might appear at first sight. This approximately nine-square expansion of the core settlement eastwards presumably followed after the granting of civic rights.

In the act of establishment, which cannot be traced for Berlin but is documented in many other cases, the territorial ruler commissioned a 'Lokator' to assemble settlers and plan the construction of the city. That the plans were carefully laid and well thought out can be seen from the clear ground design, the broad streets, and the deliberate placing of the public buildings. The rights granted with the act of establishment did not come into force for a number of years, during which the city was exempt from dues in order to build. As already explained, we may assume that this took place in Berlin around and after 1230 since the settlement and St. Nicolas' Church do not date from very much earlier. It was built over the cemetery of the original settlement and it is by no means certain that there was any continuity between the two. The sequence of events on the Spree island will have been similar. The core settlement of Cölln around the rectangular market, the fish market and church probably came into being shortly before the act of establishment. It is strikingly similar to the village green. But after the act of establishment the settlement was extended to the north and south with streets taken at right angles and rectangular urban blocks of houses.

The act of establishment applied to both cities at once. A man known as Marsilius who acted as 'scultetus' for the dual city is mentioned in the records of 1244. He may have been the 'Lokatur', who generally took the office of mayor, or at least his successor. Later the cities had separate administrations; only during the peak of economic and political power in the fourteenth and fifteenth centuries was there joint government for a time. The two cities and their markets were linked by the Mühlendamm, a dam across the Spree providing water power to drive the mills and at the same time flooding the moats. Shipping had to turn round 'von der Averspew up de Nedersprew'. Acting both as a dam and a bridge, the Mühlendamm was the main artery of the dual city for many centuries.

It was certainly already serving this function before the development of the city in the thirteenth century came to an end with the expansion on the right bank of the Spree by almost half as much again as the Berlin part of the dual city. The area laid out after 1230 ended in the north at what would later form the main east-west axis, Oderberger Strasse; this is now Rathausstrasse. In the north-east, at the tip of the ground plan triangle of the old city, stood the houses of the territorial ruler. By the middle of the century, building had commenced on the Franciscan monastery directly beside them. The whole had the appearance of a complete bourgeois community, but soon considerable further expansion was needed. This was achieved by a straight extension of the curved parallel streets across Oderberger Strasse and the creation of another nine-square expansion of housing, this time a little larger than those in the older part of the city. The middle quarter was left open for the new market. In the quarter to the east of this stood the parish church for the new district, St. Mary's. At the western end of Oderberger Strasse the Long Bridge (Lange Brücke), which led not only over the river but over marshy and initially unbuilt land, formed a second link to the Spree island.

The building of the stone city walls (recorded as finished in the year 1319 and which encircled both Berlin and Cölln) concluded the medieval development of the dual city. Five gates led to the main streets: Spandauer, Oderberger and Stralauer Strasse on the Berlin side, Köpenicker Strasse at the southern extension of Breiter Strasse and Teltower Strasse at the western end of the Fish Market on the Cölln side. The hospitals outside the gates, St. George's before the Oderberger Gate and St. Gertrude's before the Teltower, were only added later. But the Hospital of the Holy Spirit inside the city at Spandauer Gate dated from the extension period in the late thirteenth century.

Buildings

The first monumental buildings in the dual city were the churches of St. Nicolas on the Old Market in Berlin and St. Peter on the Fish Market in Cölln.[7] The churches were built of granite which had been carried into the region by the ice-age glaciers. The building technique is striking for its care and exactitude, but the hard stone offered little opportunity for richness of decoration; nor did early architecture, built to fulfil a specific purpose, require any. Both churches were originally basilicas: in Cölln a modest structure, in Berlin a rather larger one with a transept and a square choir with semi-circular apses. Both churches had broad structures several storeys high at their western ends. These were not actually towers even though they were later elevated in the manner of towers. Their defensive character made them look more like the belfries of a medieval castle and presumably they originally served such a purpose, offering a place of refuge and concealment in times of hostilities. Little had changed in the appearance of the cities by the beginning of the fourteenth century when the walls were built. The houses should be visualised as very low; only in exceptional cases were they solid.

But by 1300 other churches had been or were in the process of being built in the city, glistening in the red brick which during the last third of the thirteenth century had replaced field-stone as building material, for civic projects as well. It had been used even earlier for works commissioned by the territorial ruler, and had also been used in the Franciscan monastery begun during the first construction phase of the early thirteenth century.[8] Building continued on the church for this monastery, a vaulted basilica without a tower and with a long single choir

17

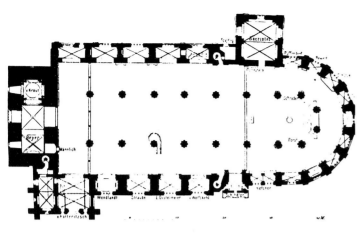

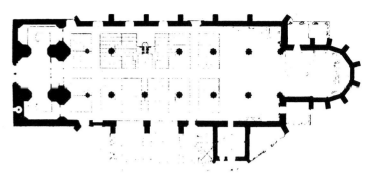

2 Ground plan of St. Nicolas' Church.

3 Ground plan of St. Mary's Church.

and polygonal eastern end. This structure lasted until the end of the century and was the last church of this conventional type in Berlin.

The second parish church in Berlin, St. Mary's in the northern district, was begun in fieldstone but finished in brick. In form it resembled another church, that of the Dominican monastery founded in 1297 and situated on the northern edge of the island city of Cölln. Like this Dominican church, St. Mary's appears to have had no western tower at first. Later the Dominican church acquired its stately towers over the western facade (resembling those in the market city of Halle) in 1536, shortly before the Reformation when the monastery was raised to the status of an electoral cathedral chapter.

The tower construction of St. Mary's at the beginning of the fifteenth century marked the end of the church's rebuilding and enlargement following its damage by fire in the fourteenth century. Devastating fires had swept through Berlin in 1376 and 1380, damaging both St. Nicolas' and St. Mary's. By then, however, St. Mary's was no longer a stone basilica but a brick hall church as well. In 1379 (between the two fires), work commenced on a grandiose new design for a long church with ambulatory and chapels. It was the earliest adaptation in the northern area of a building type developed by the Parler family of master-builders in southern Germany, and it was no doubt the result of the international trade relations which Berlin maintained at that time. But even more, this adaptation of a southern type was due to the Brandenburg region (where Berlin is situated) coming under the rulership of the Wittelsbach and

Bohemian sovereigns during the fourteenth century. Because the second fire in 1380 prevented further work, however, building did not go beyond the lower parts of the walls of the choir. It did not recommence until the end of the century when the choir was presumably finished, and the body of the church followed after the middle of the fifteenth century.

The lack of progress in the work during the late Gothic phase of building on the Berlin parish churches reflects the decline in the economic resources of the community which had been so prosperous during the fourteenth century. Probably the city never completely recovered from the damage done by the two fires. After the Mark Brandenburg came into the hands of the Hohenzollerns in 1412-17, a decline in political power was evident as well. Berlin and Cölln were the first of the cities in the Mark to lose their independence: they had to renounce their jurisdiction and staple-rights, submit to having the members of their councils confirmed in office by the territorial rulers and break all their alliances. They even had to give up the civic administration, which was only joint in certain parts. From Cölln the Hohenzollern demanded building land to the north of the Dominican monastery, on which they erected a large castle. In 1470 it became their permanent residence.

Little is known of the civic administration buildings or the town halls in Berlin and Cölln during the Middle Ages. Of the Cölln town hall we only know the site, on the Fish Market opposite the entrance to Breite Strasse. The medieval Berlin town hall stood where its modern counterpart stands, although in rather different dimensions: on the corner of Spandauer-

4 *Schlosshof* as drawn by Johann Stridbeck in 1690.

5 View from the west of the residence towns Berlin and Cölln.

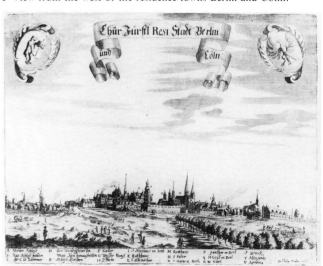

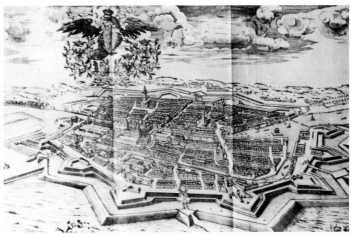

6 *Unter Den Linden* as drawn by Johann Stridbeck in 1690.

7 *Residentia Electoralis Brandenburgica* – detail from the engraving of 1688.

and Oderberger- (Rathaus-) Strasse. When the existing building was being demolished in 1860, a Gothic part was discovered among other post-medieval alterations and additions. Known as the judgement hall, it was a two-storey building, and on the ground floor was a hall open on three sides with pointed arched arcades where verdicts were pronounced. The upper storey was the council chamber. Similar buildings are to be found in several other medieval town halls in the Mark, but they are joined to larger buildings which generally served as communal shop and store. They were not free-standing, as suggested by the pavilion construction in the park of Schloss Babelsberg near Potsdam where the remains of the Gothic structure discovered in Berlin have been re-erected. There are records of a town hall on the Long Bridge ('up der nyen bruggen') for the occasional joint administration of the cities but there is no evidence of what it looked like.

Nor do we know much about medieval housing in Berlin. We may be sure that the main streets and large squares were lined with elaborate two- to three-storey houses, in which the richer citizens lived. The Renaissance facades which have been preserved in Breite Strasse in Cölln were probably not so much new buildings as adaptations of late medieval houses, and the same applies to the gabled houses facing the street and the houses on several axes with eaves, of which the Ribbeck house is one of the earliest (1624). These were created by merging two or more older plots, a common practice in the seventeenth century. The old plots were very narrow and the gable fronts on the street were hardly more than three or four window

breadths wide. Archaeological work enabled one of the late Gothic residential houses, which belonged to the family Winz or Wiens, to be fully reconstructed in plan in 1954-56.[10] The house was two storeys high and stood with a three-axis gable on Oderberger strasse. Behind the house in the courtyard stood a second building with vaulted rooms; there was also a separate kitchen house built of brick containing not only the kitchen and pantry but a dining-room with a reticulated ceiling. In the upper storey were the bathrooms. These detached solid kitchen houses were frequent in Berlin. They gave greater protection against fire, and this suggests that most of the residential building in the late Middle Ages was still half-timbered.

In the sixteenth century building activity in Berlin concentrated on the alterations to the Hohenzollern residence on the Spree island. The building, modelled on the Wettin residences in Torgau, Wittenberg and Dresden from where the artists and architects were drawn, became a magnificent Renaissance palace. In the 1540s, after the establishment of the Reformation in Brandenberg as well, Saxon influence replaced the older Franconian-Nuremberg tradition. Caspar Theiss, who is regarded as a pupil of the Torgau master-builder Konrad Krebs, built the Second House ('Zweites Haus'), the south wing of the palace, in a style similar to that of Krebs' 'Johann-Friedrich-Bau' at Schloss Hartenfels: in three storeys with round oriels at the corners, spiral columns on the courtyard front and a gallery on the street frontage. In the second half of the sixteenth century Italian artists and architects such as Chiaramella de Gandino, Rochus von Lynar,

7a *Residentia Electoralis Brandenburgica* – a bird's eye view of Berlin. Engraving by Johann Bernhard Schultz in 1688.

8 The Leipziger city gate in Berlin designed by Johann Arnold Nering. Engraving by Wolff.

9 Spandauerstrasse as drawn by Johann Stridbeck in 1690.

10 Mühlendamm as drawn by Johann Stridbeck in 1690.

Peter Niuron worked on the palace, and after 1600 Giovanni Battista Sala worked there also. After 1640 we find Dutch or Dutch-trained master-builders such as Johann Gregor Memhardt, Michael Mattias Smids, Rutger von Langerfeld, Cornelis Ryckwaert and Johann Arnold Nering who enriched the palace building by making additions to it and attempting to give conclusive accents to the picture which had gradually emerged. But it was not until Andreas Schlüter came to work that this was achieved, and then only by the sacrifice of the Renaissance form to his grandiose Baroque design.

Extensions

Among the Dutch masters whom Friedrich Wilhelm, the Great Elector, summoned to Berlin, Memhardt and the garden architect Michael Hanff, who had learned from Le Nôtre, turned the northern part of the Spree island (which until then had been a marshy waste) into a pleasure garden. Memhardt's map of the two electoral residence cities Berlin and Cölln on the Spree already shows the garden. The map also shows the route to the Elector's hunting ground, the Tiergarten, which was laid out to the west of the castle across the Spree and lined with two triple rows of linden trees. This avenue of linden trees marked the beginning of the Baroque development of Berlin.

When he came to the throne in 1640, however, the Great Elector found his capital in ruins. The events of the Thirty Years' War had halved the number of occupied houses and inhabitants of Berlin and Cölln, and it was not until ten years later that the Great Elector and his consort finally took up residence in Berlin. However, measures to expand the city and rebuild it as a fortress had begun earlier under the direction of Memhardt, the leading architect and engineer. The copper engraving published by Johann Bernhard Schultz in 1688 gives a bird's-eye view of Berlin and shows it as a fortress city after the Dutch pattern, with a star-shaped ground plan to the fortifications, surrounded by moats and walls, with six gates each between two bastions. Leipziger Tor, the gate on the south-west side, acquired some distinction. It was the work of Johann Arnold Nering, the most distinguished of the Dutch masters born in Wesel on the Lower Rhine.[12]

Nering gave the old city and its buildings major new accents. He added arcades to the palace (around 1680), new colonnades of shops to the Mühlendamm (1687) made an imposing addition to the town hall (1692-95), and rebuilt the wooden Long Bridge in stone (1692-95). He also built for private customers, not only members of the nobility like the minister von Danckelmann, but for bourgeois families as well. Other Dutch masters engaged at court did the same. The 'Friedrichsgracht' on the widened bank of the western arm of the Spree in Cölln looks like a water frontage in the Dutch manner. Some of the facades with their strict division in the Palladian classical manner are ascribed to Michael Matthias Smids, who lived not far from here (near the lock).[13]

The palace Nering built for Eberhard von Danckelmann was not within the dual city area but in a new district to the west of Cölln. The marshy land had been drained by the regulation of the arm of the Spree, creating building land for the new city of Friedrichswerder[14] which was given civic rights in 1662 and included in the new fortification ring. Friedrichswerder was not the only new city area to emerge during the reign of the Great Elector. To the north of the linden avenue beyond the fortifications, Dorotheenstadt was laid out, largely to house Hugenots who had fled from France. In the bird's-eye view by Schultz in 1688 it can already be seen in two parallel flights of streets and a cross-shaped church which is ascribed to Rutger von Langerfeld. During the reign of the Great Elector's son, who had himself crowned King of Prussia in 1701, Friedrichstadt (the city named after him) was laid out after 1688 to the south. The widespread network of right-angled streets was gradually built up by 1738, but it was also constantly being extended by prolonging the main streets. The north-south axis (Friedrichstrasse) went from one of the bridges over the Spree (Weidendammer Brücke) north of Dorotheenstadt and ended far in the south at a round place, the Rondel (Mehringplatz). Leipziger Strasse, which led from Cölln, became the east-west axis. It was taken far over the line intended as the western border of the district (the curving Mauerstrasse) and continued west to the 'Oktogon' (Leipziger Platz) directly on the Tiergarten. And the linden avenue also received an extension in the form of an open square, known as the 'Quarrée' (Pariser Platz), with the Brandenburg Gate. On the basis of these axes and squares in the extensions to the west of the old dual city, the Baroque royal capital was built; henceforth it was to overshadow the old medieval city.

Translated from the German by Eileen Martin

11 Friedrichsgracht as drawn by Johann Stridbeck in 1690.

Ernst Badstübner:
Art historian, born 1931. Studied with Richard Hamann, took his doctorate degree with Edgar Lehmann; worked on art topography and preservation. Publications on the architecture of the Middle Ages (Church Architecture of the Monastic Reform Period, monograph) and of the nineteenth century, and Christian iconography. Guest lecturer on medieval architecture at the Humboldt University in Berlin.

Notes

1 A.V. Müller, 'Berlin vor 800 Jahren, Berlin 1968 in: *Berlin una Brandenburg (Handbuch der historischen Stätten* Vol. 10 Stuttgart 1973.

2 W. Volk, *Berlin: Hauptstadt der DDR. Historische Strasen und Plätze heute* 5th ed. Berlin 1977.

3 E. Reinbacher, *Die älteste Baugeschichte der Nikolaikirche in Alt-Berlin* Berlin 1963.

4 H-D.Kahl, *Slawen and Deutsche in der Brandenburgischen Geschichte des 12. Jahrhunderts* Cologne/Graz 1964.

5 E. Müller-Mertens, 'Untersuchungen zur Geschichte der Brandenburgischen Städte im Mittelalter' in *Wiss.Zeitschr.d.Humboldt-Universität Berlin, gesellschafts- und sprachwiss. Reihe,* Vol.5 (1955-56) and Vol.6 (1956-57); ibid., 'Die Entstehung der Stadt Berlin' in *Berliner Heimat* Vol.9 1960; J. Schultze, *Die Mark Brandenburg* Vol.1, Berlin 1961; W.H. Fritze, 'Das Vordringen deutscher Herrschaft in Teltow und Barnim' in *Jahrbuch für Brandenburg. Landesgeschichte,* Vol.22 1971.

6 J. Siedler, *Märkischer Städtebau im Mittelalter* Berlin 1914.

7 G. Leh, *Die St. Nikolai-Kirche zu Berlin* Berlin 1961; E. Lehmann, 'Bemerkungen zu den beiden Vorgängerbauten der spätgotischen Nikolaikirche zu Berlin' in ref. no.3; W. Nitschke, 'Die beiden Vorgängerbauten der spätgotischen Nikolaikirche zu Berlin' in ref. no. 3; G. Schade, 'St. Nikolai in Berlin: Ein baugeschichtlicher Deutungsversuch des Hallenchores mit Kapellenkranz' in *Jahrbuch für Brandenburg: Landesgeschichte,* Vol.17 (1966); K. Koziol, *Kleine Chronik der St.Petri-Kirche zu Berlin* Berlin 1965.

8 G. Bronisch, *Die Franziskaner-Klosterkirche in Berlin,* Berlin 1933; A. Schmoll gen. Eisenwerth, *Das Kloster Chorin und die askanische Architektur in der Mark Brandenburg 1260 bis 1320* Berlin 1961.

9 E. Badstübner, *Die Marienkirche zu Berlin,* 3rd ed. Berlin 1979.

10 E. Reinbacher, 'Uber die mittelalterliche Bebauung des Grundstückes Hoher Steinweg 15 in Berlin' in *Ausgrabungen und Funde* Vol.4 (1956).

11 M. Osborn, *Berlin,* 2. Aufl. Leipzig 1926; A. Geyer, *Geschichte des Schlosses zu Berlin,* Vol.1. *Die kurfürstliche Zeit bis zum Jahre 1698* Berlin 1936.

12 St. Hirzel, *Arnold Nering, ein märkischer Baumeister,* Dresden 1924 (thesis); G. Fritsch, *Die Burgkirche zu Königsberg in Preussen und ihre Beziehungen zur Neringforschung,* Leipzig, 1930.

13 *Schicksale deutscher Baudenkmale im zweiten Weltkrieg,* Vol.1, *Berlin –Hauptstadt der DDR* (H. Drescher) Berlin 1978; M. Rudolph, 'Friedrichsgracht Nr.58' in *Jahrbluch für Brandenberg. Landesgeschichte* Vol.15 (1964) and Vol.16 (1965).

14 W. Erman, *Berlin anno 1690. Zwanzig Ansichten aus Johann Stridbecks des Jüngeren Skizzenbuch* Berlin 1881.

15 H. Reuther, *Barock in Berlin* Berlin 1969.

12 The Fishmarket in Cölln as engraved by Georg Rosenberg in 1785.

13 New Market in Berlin as engraved by Georg Rosenberg in 1785.

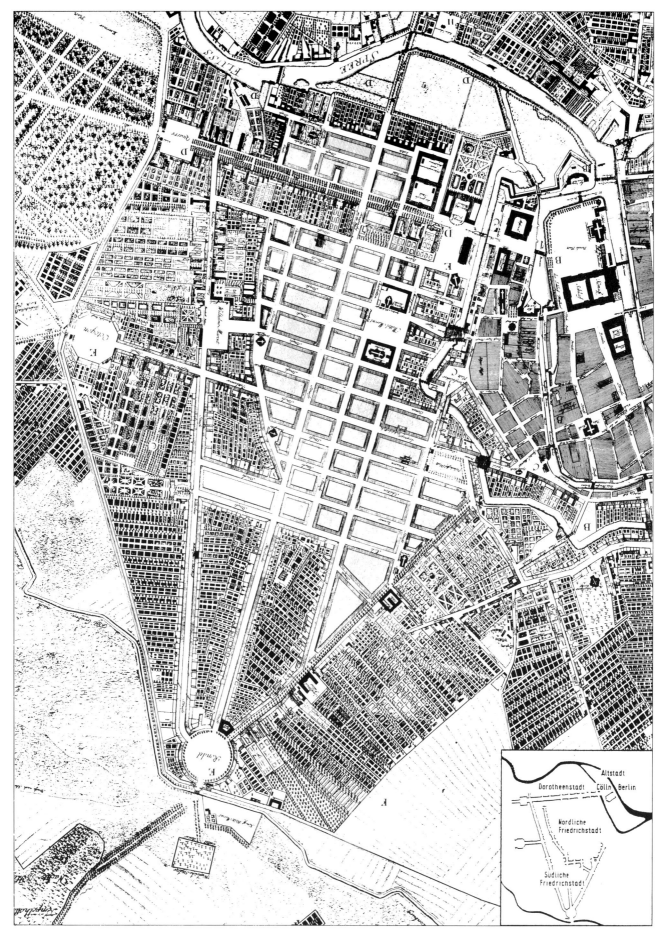

1 Southern Friedrichstadt, 1748, Schmettau.

David Leatherbarrow
Friedrichstadt – A Symbol of Toleration

Friedrichstadt was the largest seventeenth-eighteenth century suburb of Berlin and was named after its founder, Friedrich Wilhelm, the Great Elector of Brandenburg. Like other cities named after their founders – Rome, Alexandria and Washington – Friedrichstadt represented its founder's conception of the best policy of public order. This was the policy of toleration. My purpose in examining the early history of Friedrichstadt is to interpret the historical meaning of toleration and to evaluate the Great Elector's estimation of its merit. In contemporary architectural theory, the word 'pluralism' has replaced the policy known as toleration in the seventeenth and eighteenth centuries. An evaluation of the older term, as it was realised in built urban form, will enable us to discern the shortcomings of its twentieth-century equivalent.

The term 'toleration' is seldom used in contemporary urban theory for purposes of characterising a city. One finds it more commonly applied in political science to name a certain form of social being: 'patient forbearance in the presence of something disliked or disapproved of'.[1] Application of the term to the study of built cities is acceptable in view of the etymological connection between the original Greek signification of political science as *episteme politike* and the built city as the *polis*. Both *episteme politike* and the *polis* are representations of the order of the political community, originally called in Greek the *koinoina politikon*, and more radically political existence, first named *zoon politikon*. A term such as toleration can thus be used to characterise both the built form and the political idea of a city.

But even in contemporary political science the term toleration is not used very frequently. The sentiments once expressed in this way are not represented among the group signified by the very common term 'liberalism'. The history of this term is not, however, very ancient. It seems that it has been in currency since the second decade of the nineteenth century when a party of the Spanish Parliament of 1812 called itself the *Liberales*.[2] As the policy of the *Liberales,* liberalism signified the doctrine of constitutionalism, which was then conceived in opposition to that favouring restoration. But today the word is not used in that sense, its significance in contemporary discourse exceeding the original doctrine and thus too broad to permit its use to analyse pre-nineteenth-century political or urban problems. The word 'toleration', however, has not suffered the same extension and attenuation and can be used with some precision.

The practice of toleration emerged as a social policy after the experience of the religious wars of the sixteenth and seventeenth centuries; more specifically, out of the insight that 'the truth of Christendom could not be saved by the churches exterminating each other for the sake of dogma, the insight that the churches must somehow live together in one society'.[3] A great seventeenth-eighteenth century advocate of toleration was the English free-thinker John Toland, whose interpretation was presented in a number of publications, the most famous being *Christianity Not Mysterious* of 1696. But the work of most interest is *An Account of the Courts of Prussia and Hannover,* published in 1705; in this short piece Toland celebrated the King of Prussia's encouragement of religious freedom, and called his residentiary city, Berlin, a city of toleration. A review of his description will serve as an introduction to this account of the foundation and early history of its principle suburb, Friedrichstadt.

A Tolerant City

According to Toland, the happy prosperity of late seventeenth-century Berlin could be explained by the conspicuous presence of three civic conditions: the rise in industrial production and economic achievement that followed the remarkable population growth in the years immediately after the end of the Thirty Years War; the liberty of conscience enjoyed by the residents; and the availability of houses for all newcomers. There appears to be no inherent order in Toland's list of 'civic conditions' and for our purposes it is necessary that the list be reorganised. First we will examine the second of these conditions, then the third and lastly the first. This order is an abstraction of the consequent stages of the institutionalisation of political order, which was in this case the order of the tolerant city.

Toland reported that strangers to the Mark Brandenburg were not afraid to settle in Berlin because they had been assured of the agreeable social manners of the inhabitants. The development of differences of opinion into acts of aggression, commonplace in other European capitals, was uncommon in Berlin. Despite their differences, the citizens Toland observed peacefully tolerated one another. Newcomers feared for neither their estates nor their lives because the practice of forbearance was universally adhered to. Lutherans were amicable neighbours to Calvinists, Socianians patiently suffered Mennonites and Aryans endured Jews.

The sacred architecture of the city mirrored this social form. According to Toland, church builders purposefully neglected denominational iconography by abstracting traditional signs and marks of distinction from the visible face of their constructions. No edifice was designed to compete with others for public recognition, and the policy of toleration was thus represented throughout the city. Even the King himself exemplified this custom. He professed the Calvinist faith, but did not force his convictions upon his subjects, the majority of whom were Lutherans. The state, personified in the King, separated itself from the churches. The highest measure of civil cohesion and political unanimity – that bonding of individuals in a common cause on the basis of a recognised common nature that Cicero called *concordia* – was not what characterised late seventeenth-century Berlin; but neither was its opposite, *dissensio*. Those who gathered on the banks of the Spree tolerated one another, and in so doing contributed to the city's welfare.

The next 'cause' of Berlin's success in the years after the Peace of Westphalia to be considered is the availability of

2 Houses in southern Friedrichstadt, seventeenth century, painter unknown.

houses for newcomers to the city. Although Toland does not name the houses to which he refers, he is probably alluding to the 300 new dwellings built by Johann Arnold Nering. Nering was an engineer trained in military architecture and civil engineering in Holland who received the title 'Ingenieur Oberst' in Brandenburg in 1685. Three years later he laid out Berlin's second suburb, Friedrichstadt, as a southern extension of Dorotheenstadt, which was built nearly 20 years earlier and named after the Great Elector's second wife Dorothea. Along the projected streets of Friedrichstadt, Nering built rows of houses for the expected newcomers as well as for those who chose to leave their ruined houses in the old city. These houses, like the churches Toland described, were built without marks of distinction. Nering's architecture has been called Palladian, presumably because of his Dutch training; but this attribution, based as it is on available and familiar terms of architectureal historiography, obscures the historical meaning of these houses. In the notable absence of stylistic or decorative differentiation between the houses, one detects a connection between architectural style and the tolerant manner of the Berliners.

The third and last factor contributing to Berlin's prosperity mentioned by Toland is the remarkable population growth that followed the end of the war. The figures are, in fact, extraordinary. In 1450, more than 250 years before Friedrichstadt was projected, the population of Berlin and Cölln combined was approximately 6,000. By 1600, the population had risen to 8,000. By 1618, the year of the outbreak of the Thirty Years War, the numbers of the city had jumped to 12,000. When the war ended the number of citizens had dropped to 6,000. But the extraordinary figure is the next one: by 1713, the year of the King of Prussia's death, Berlin's population had increased ten-fold to 60,000. The people that constituted this number were those that Toland observed had contributed to Berlin's 'happy prosperity' in the early eighteenth century.

The explanation for this extraordinary increase in numbers is the same simple explanation as that of the 'liberty of conscience enjoyed by the Berliners' and the undifferentiated style of the new houses in Friedrichstadt: it is the policy of toleration. By 1687 45 per cent of those living in Berlin were French Huguenots, and by that same date 20,000 persecuted Protestants had emigrated to Prussia from France and Holland. The explanation for the great increase in numbers during these years is the Great Elector's offer in the Edict of Potsdam of a 'sure and free retreat in all the lands and provinces in our dominion'[4] to all who were suffering for their religion under Louis XIV. This edict was issued in 1685 as a response to Louis' revocation of the Edict of Nantes, and is perhaps the clearest and most concise statement of the Great Elector's policy of toleration, and analogously his programme for the building of Friedrichstadt.

The Edict of Potsdam also has been called the essential factor in the Great Elector's 'system of home colonisation'.[5] This is a handy attribution for historians and readers familiar with the practice of colonisation, but is also one that is acceptable in the case of Friedrichstadt only if used carefully. The range of meanings commonly implied by 'colonisation' stretches from the act of establishing a settlement in a new land to the act of 'civilising' recalcitrant natives. The Great Elector's 'system of home colonisation' is highly specific and must be differentiated within the range of these meanings. The establishment of a colony involves the work of reconciling the colonial's vision – whether a remembered or a projected vision – of the new settlement with the physical conditions of the new land. The 'civilisation' of a native population involves this work of reconciliation and something more: the conversion of a people designated variously as primitives, barbarians or aborigines to a way of life unknown to them. The work of conversion presupposes having the knowledge of the 'best' or 'right' way of life which, when substituted for the rough or wild way of the natives, will effect their betterment. Thus, conversion is connected with education and improvement. This component of the colonisation practiced in the sixteenth century was connected with the Greek idea of *paideia* (the art of 'turning around') and with the Christian idea of *conversio ad Christi* (the turning of non-Christians round to Christ). The men who colonised foreign lands believed it was necessary to convert or turn the natives around to their conception of the best way of life. The art of turning around was, and in fact still is, practiced in a number of different ways. The surprising inventiveness of the colonial's imagination in this connection precludes the listing of all these ways; but an indication of the range seems of some help. These ways extend from the teaching of those who are anxious to learn, to the persuasion of those hesitant to follow, to the extermination of those determined to stubbornly keep their old ways. But no matter which techniques are exercised, no matter how ardent the colonial's 'humanitarian' zeal, the act of conversion in this form of colonisation presupposes the belief in the necessity of 'spreading' the 'best way of life' throughout the ecumene.

The 'colonisation' practiced by the Great Elector in Prussia had nothing whatsoever to do with this idea of conversion. He had neither techniques for 'turning around' nor an idea of the 'best way of life' to which all encountered should conform. The Edict of Potsdam suggests an opposite policy. Newcomers to the dominions of the Great Elector were at full liberty to dispose themselves as they chose. All French and Dutch *emigrés* were looked upon and treated as natural subjects of the land and were judged, in all cases, equal to native Germans. The Elector's policy was to act in a friendly and compassionate way to all. No imposition of any kind was made upon a stranger's way of life. A newcomer had neither to forget his old ways nor conform to new ways; according to Toland, every way was tolerated.

The government of Brandenburg permitted the free importation of foreign goods by all incoming settlers. Free transportation to the Electorate was provided, as was government money and building materials for the construction of new houses and business premises. In addition, houses standing vacant were freely offered to newcomers who preferred not to build. The new population was exempted from normal taxation for six years and was allowed to represent itself in legal disputes with elected members from its own community. Finally, those who settled in Prussia were allowed to practice their religion without suffering state attempts at conversion or fear of persecution. The description of the Great

Elector's programme for rebuilding his territory after the Thirty Years War as 'home colonisation' is appropriate if the idea of 'turning the strangers around' is excluded.

The Great Elector was not, of course, the only late seventeenth century ruler to encourage religious freedom or to favour toleration, for this conception had currency in Germany, Holland and England, too. However, he was perhaps the only leader of his time to respond to the religious wars in this way with absolute conviction and consistent practical application. The site, or physical context, on which the Great Elector represented the body of ideas adumbrated in the Edict of Potsdam was the area round the old cities of Berlin and Cölln, the territory he named Dorotheenstadt and Friedrichstadt. The design and building of these suburbs was not carried out by native Berliners or Germans but by Dutch architects, engineers, gardeners and builders. The Elector collected this team during his stay in Holland before his rise to the Electorate.

Holland and Berlin

In 1634, sixteen years after the outbreak of the Thirty Years War and a hundred years after John of Leyden, a self-appointed King of Sion, and his band of fanatical Anabaptists besieged the Westphalian town of Münster, young Friedrich Wilhelm was sent to Leyden with an ardent Calvinist named Leuchtman as his guardian to escape the danger of the recent conflicts in Brandenburg and to begin his university training. He had been away from Berlin since 1626, when at the age of six he began his stay at the Oder fortress of Cüstrin and his study of the rudimentary habits of the aristocratic life (riding, fencing, shooting) and foreign languages (Latin, Dutch, French and Polish). After his time at Cüstrin, he spent some years travelling throughout his father's dominions, being warmly received by his future subjects, and visiting those lands outside Brandenburg which were accessible through firmly-established diplomatic relations. But his formal training as a statesman began with his stay in Holland where he discovered the best form of political order.

The University of Leyden was founded in 1575 and was established by Prince Henry of Orange as an expression of 'the gratitude entertained by the people of Holland and Zeland for the heroism of the citizens'[6] in their resistance to the attack made upon their city by the Spanish army. The stamp of the House of Orange on the University of Leyden made it particularly appealing to the Elector of Brandenburg. The Houses of Orange, Brandenburg and Palatinate had been interconnected through marriages during the preceding half of a century and by sending the fourteen-year-old to Leyden, the Elector was certain of the kind of education his son would receive.

The details of Friedrich Wilhelm's university course have not been recorded but are nevertheless sufficient to reconstruct the influences the Protestant city had on him. He is said to have acquired considerable knowledge both in languages and in the physical sciences, and was especially interested in military tactics — an interest which in his later years was to have considerable value and consistent application. But he also showed a strong interest in religion, and steadily pursued theological studies. One modern biographer has written that at this time Friedrich Wilhelm's 'Protestant feelings were strengthened'.[7] Leyden was the place where he made strong contacts with communicants of the Reformed church. His course of studies was one that was approved by seventeenth-century Calvinists and was one designed to direct students in the Calvinist way of life.

Perhaps the two most famous Calvinists to spend time in Leyden while Friedrich Wilhelm was there were Pierre Jurieu and Pierre Bayle. Both Jurieu and Bayle claimed to represent Calvin's ideas, but as they matured and published their own works it became clear that there was an unbridgeable distance between their conceptions of Calvinist orthodoxy. In their last years they became bitter opponents: Jurieu labelled Bayle an atheist and Bayle described Jurieu's political ideas as intolerant. It is difficult to determine when Friedrich Wilhelm met Bayle, but the latter became attached to the House of Brandenburg sometime after the 1630s. Friedrich Wilhelm's first cousin, called Friedrich de Dohna, employed Bayle as a secretary in the 1660s and 1670s. Bayle himself planned to move to Berlin in 1687 but never did.

In 1686 Bayle published his *Commentaire philosophique sur ces paroles de Jésus Christ 'Constrains-les d'entrer'*, the most profound and thoroughgoing argument in favour of complete religious toleration published in the seventeenth century. This work appeared one year after the Great Elector issued the Edict of Potsdam. Bayle's publication was a sharper statement of some of the same ideas contained in the Great Elector's Edict, and there is no doubt that the Elector's policy of toleration was identical to that of the leading figures of Dutch Calvinism. It will be seen that his ways of representing this policy in built urban form were also identical to Dutch examples.

Rebuilding Berlin

Friedrich Wilhelm reluctantly returned to Berlin in 1638. His father was ill and, anticipating his own death, he called the heir to the Electorate home so that he could prepare himself for his new position. However, despite the apparent urgency of the situation, the young prince did not immediately return and had to be called repeatedly (three times in nine months) during which time he invited local architects, engineers, gardeners and builders to join him in the Brandenburg capital. He knew that the talents they possessed were not easily had in Berlin, and imagined that if he was to realise the city he thought best, the importation of personnel capable of managing the task was necessary. Fifteen months after his return to Berlin Friedrich Wilhelm's father died and he was named the Elector. The tasks immediately facing him were numerous, namely, ending the then 22-year-old war, and rebuilding his residentiary city; both were equally pressing and in need of speedy execution.

One year after receiving his title, the Elector passed a number of laws pertaining to future building in Berlin regulating the kind and quality of all new construction. Specifically, the building of barns and pigsties on main streets was prohibited, as was the drainage of sewage and rain water into open ditches and public routes. There is no evidence to suggest these practices were uncommon before the outbreak of the Thirty Years War. On the contrary, it seems that the fifteenth- and sixteenth-century city permitted the coincidence of domestic, mercantile and stabling properties. Perhaps the significant change effected by the war was the lack of interest in property management: the Berliners had better things to do than clean the streets. Thus, the first task the new Elector executed was the cleaning of the city.

During this time he also began applying himself to the improvement of his palace on the opposite bank of the Spree, in Cölln. Following his activity there, this district came to be called Friedrichwerder, but the site had always been known as the resident Elector's home territory and was architecturally distinguished as such. There had been a palace there since the

3 J Stridbeck, view of the internal court of the old Schloss, Friedrichswerder, 1690-91. (Ph Landesbildstelle Berlin)

4 J Memhardt, plan of Berlin and Cölln, 1647. (Ph Landesbildstelle Berlin)

middle of the sixteenth century, when Konrad Krebs, the architect to Joachim II and designer of the great Schloss Hartenfels, built one. But a hundred years later, when Friedrich Wilhelm moved in, the building was in a bad state of repair. The Elector made some improvements to the interior of the old Schloss and added two new parts: the wing of private apartments to the south along the Spree, and the famous Alabaster Hall in the wing across the old courtyard.

The Elector's response to the sad state of his city was also represented in his building of an extensive 'Lustgarten' ('pleasure garden') in Friedrichwerder. Begun in 1645, it was not open for the use of the Berliners, though it was publicly visible and thus constituted an expression of the Elector's conception of the order of a residence city. His gardener was Michael Hanff, the son of Hans Hanff, who was employed by the previous Elector. Hanff's first job was to remove the old trees and wild shrubs that had grown out of control in the land behind the Schloss since the beginning of the war. After the land had been cleared it was ploughed, fertilised and prepared for a new flower garden which comprised the first of two large, flat terraces that made up the first section of the 'Lustgarten'; its plan was of a rectangle divided into quarters and lined along its central axis with box trees. These quarters were decorated with the name and official title of the Elector and his wife, as well as a pair of eagles. In the centre of the flower garden was a water basin made of unwrought rock, in the middle of which

was a great marble statue of Neptune.

Modern commentators have described the gardening of Michael Hanff as 'inspired by André Le Notre'.[8] There is, however, no evidence to demonstrate that Hanff ever saw a garden by the French master; considering both the form of his garden and the politics of his employer, one doubts that if he had knowledge of Le Notre's style or principles he would have applied them in Berlin. The differences between the politics of Louis XIV and the Great Elector have already been indicated, but differences between Le Notre's axial planning and rigid geometry and Hanff's design are also distinct for another reason. Hanff's garden contained representations of eagles and Neptune, both emblems of non-French peoples: the eagle had been associated with Germany since Emperor Charles V used it to represent the German Empire (it had been previously used to represent the Roman Empire), and by the time the Electors of Brandenburg used Neptune to represent the Duchy of Prussia, it had been associated with Holland since the Dutch mastery of the seas during the reign of the House of Orange. The union of the Houses of Orange and Brandenburg was obvious in the coupling of the names of Friedrich Wilhelm of Brandenburg and Louise Henriette of Orange, but was also apparent in the joining of the eagle with Neptune. Together they symbolised a united front against Louis XIV. If there is a similarity between Hanff's garden and the gardens of the famous Frenchman, it is only a dubious formal similarity. The meanings of the

5 J Stridbeck, view of the Berlin Lustgarten toward the Schloss, 1691. (Ph Landesbildstelle Berlin)

6 J Stridbeck, view of Berlin Lustgarten with the Lusthaus on the right and the Pommeranzenhaus at the end of the axis, 1690. (Ph Landesbildstelle Berlin)

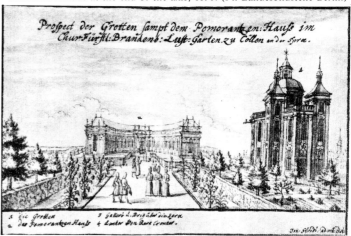

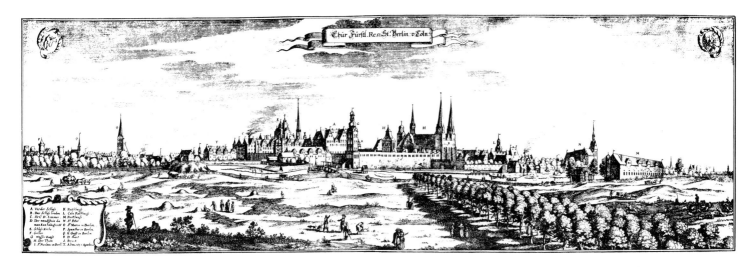

7 M Merian, view of Berlin with Linden Allee in the foreground, 1650.

gardeners were different.

The flower garden was connected to a sunken garden by a descending stairway of seven steps. At the bottom of the stairway was a marble statue of Pomona, the Roman goddess of fruit trees, usually orange and lime or linden trees. She had been appropriated by the Dutch and where she stood was taken as a sign of their influence. Thus, Friedrich Wilhelm's affection for the country of his education was apparent in the second part of the garden, as it was in the first. The plan of the sunken garden was a long rectangle, divided into three squares, each of those quartered (similar to the flower garden). The paths through the middle part were covered with arcaded elm trees, while the paths of the other parts were lined with *ligustrum* or privet. Both elm trees and privet were common in Holland. There were 42 statues in the sunken garden; 11 were marble figures, 2 were busts made of stone and 29 others were made of lead. Sadly, the identity of these figures does not seem to have been recorded. This is a pity because their names would doubtlessly aid any interpretation of the garden. Finally, in the centre of the middle square there was a tree garden made of orange trees, in the centre of which was a pool and a fountain. A bird house was supposed to be built, but never was.

On the east side of the sunken garden was a herb garden. It seems that it was laid out by Hanff (maybe J G Memhardt), but after 1656 it became the responsibility of a man called Johann Elsholtz, a botanist and the Elector's personal physician. He was a German by birth who trained both in his native country and in Italy. Elsholtz published a number of books which treated subjects such as chemistry, blood transfusion, palmistry, the manufacture of phosphorus and the physiology of sight. There seems little doubt that he was a Hermeticist and an alchemist. He purported to have made Rhine gold and offered to sell it to people decorating their houses and grottoes. Presumably his products brightened the interiors of the grottoes in the Berlin 'Lustgarten'. His work in Berlin was wide-ranging, but he was paid for his work in the herb garden. His achievements there contributed to the Elector's good health.

On the west side of the sunken garden there was a water garden with walls in the form of miniature dikes resembling typical land formations in Holland. Further to the west was a line of caves or grottoes which backed onto a line of trees and the bank of the Spree. The passage north through the sunken garden led to a stairway of seven steps ending at the foot of a row of 700 linden trees encircling the whole of the north part of the garden. They were purchased in Holland and presented to the Great Elector by a man called Dogers. Thus, the garden had references to Holland in its centre and at its periphery.

In the northern-most part of the garden was the kitchen garden. This, too, became the responsibility of Elsholtz. However, by the 1660s its site was taken for the ground floor of the great 'Pommeranzenhaus'. This piece was built by Johann

8 Berlin and Linden Allee in 1692, painter unknown.

27

9 J Stridbeck, Linden Allee looking toward the Tiergarten, with Dorotheenstadt on the right and the beginning of Friedrichstadt on the left, 1690. (Ph Landesbildstelle Berlin)

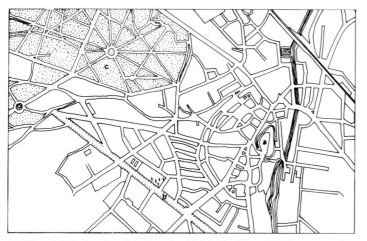

10 Cleve, 1978, showing: (a) Altstadt, (b) Linden Allee, (c) Tiergarten, after Murray.

11 Cleve in the early eighteenth century, showing the urban design of Moritz: (a) Altstadt, (b) Linden Allee (c) Tiergarten, after Murray.

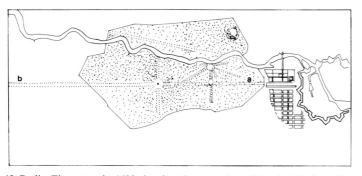

12 Berlin Tiergarten in 1698 showing the extension of the (a) Linden Allee toward (b) Charlottenburg, after 'Berlin und Seine Baukunst'.

Gregor Memhardt, the author of the first plan of Berlin who was born in Linz but taught architecture and civil engineering in Holland. Memhardt was also responsible for the design and construction of the famous 'Lusthaus' finished in 1647. The architect's Dutch training was obvious on the exterior of this building; it was unlike anything in Berlin and must have represented to the Berliners and immigrating Frenchmen the Elector's associations with Holland. Typical Dutch features of the 'Lusthaus' included elongated giant pilasters on the facade, high windows with heavy garlands, and brick walls with ashlar construction. In plan, four octagonal rooms were set round a small square hall, and in section there were two towers in front and a dome.[9] On the ground floor was a grotto. The Elector's Dutch wife involved herself in the building of this room. It was decorated with shells and unusual stones, and contained a 'kleine vexir-Springbrunnen' (small water spray trick). The grotto was also the place where the Elector and Electress took their evening meals. In the dome at the top of the 'Lusthaus' was a gallery, and from there the Elector could see the whole of his city and far into the extent of his Electorate, Brandenburg. Thus, when overlooking his dominions the Elector was standing in the middle of a Dutch garden. His position could be characterised as observing the city from the Dutch point of view, the distinctive nature of which will be indicated in our review of the Elector's other designs for the city; namely, Linden Allee, Dorotheenstadt and Friedrichstadt.

The western end of Linden Allee appears on Memhardt's 1648 plan of Berlin. At that date it ran from the 'Hundsbrücke' (dog's bridge) to the edge of the Elector's hunting grounds, the Tiergarten. It was 60 meters wide and 1,000 meters long. Along its length stretched six rows of 1,000 linden trees and 1,000 walnut trees. The Allee, or Galerie as it was also called, was laid out by three garden architects: Michael Hanff (the designer of the 'Lusgarten'), Johannes Grünberg and Hans Dressler. These three were supervised by Johann Moritz, the 'Statthalter' of Cleve. Moritz was known to the Elector since the time when the latter was married to Louise Henriette in Cleve, and had been there since 1644 when he returned to Europe from Brazil where he had been in service to the Dutch Republic. While he was working in that colony, Moritz involved himself in urban design and gardening. Reports attribute fabulous castles, pleasure gardens and public avenues to him. Although these reports are somewhat dubious, there is no doubt that when he returned to Cleve, which was then part of the Electorate of Brandenburg, Moritz spent considerable time and state funds in civic design. During the last years of the Thirty Years War he transformed Cleve 'from a wretched place to a flourishing residential town. He put up avenues... artificial mounds and a series of country houses.'[10] He designed a Tiergarten outside the old city and planted a Linden Allee between a nearby park and Cleveberg. Allees such as this were not as common in northern Europe as they are now, but the rows of linden trees must have reminded Friedrich Wilhelm and his new wife of their earlier days in Holland. When they returned to Berlin they employed Moritz to plant a similar Allee between their palace, the Tiergarten and distant Lütze, later Charlottenburg.

Since there is no plan of Berlin before Memhardt's, it is impossible to know with certainty whether there was a path or a road running to the Tiergarten leading from the new Allee, although it would seem that there was. The Tiergarten had been used for hunting by both the rulers and the citizens of Berlin since the earliest days of the city and in the beginning of the seventeenth century there was a settlement at Lütze. On La

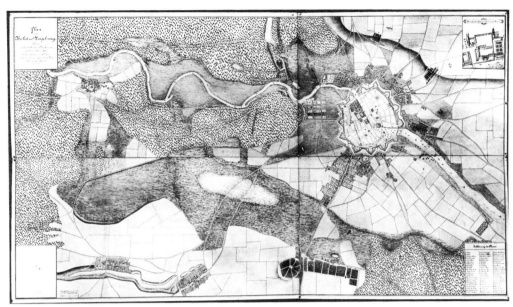

13 La Vigne, plan of Berlin and Dorotheenstadt, 1685. (Ph Landesbildstelle Berlin).

Vigne's plan of 1685 there is a small road perpendicular and south of Linden Allee which because Friedrichstrasse. It is not improbable that a similar road antedated Linden Allee.

Moreover, this supposed history of Linden Allee does not contradict Dutch strategies of urban development, that is, pragmatic, modest and responsive to existing physical conditions; it conforms to Friedrich Wilhelm's conception of the best form of public order, the policy of toleration. Just as the Great Elector's political policy differed from the Sun King's policy of persecution, so did his city, and a comparison between Berlin and Versailles is instructive.

The most obvious difference between the two cities is that the centre of the Schloss at Berlin was not the starting point of the Linden Allee, whereas the centre of the Palace at Versailles was the starting point, the *focal point* of the *Grand Allée*. There is neither a perspective view nor a privileged position in the urban form of Berlin, whereas in Versailles one finds both. Louis XIV occupied a privileged position in Versailles: from where he stood, the landscape could be seen in perfect order. The whole place made sense from the centre of the rear facade of his palace. It was not just that Louis was in control of the landscape, but that the landscape could be controlled (visually) from where he stood, the perspective point of view. This is what the garden was designed for, to represent an individual's control over the landscape.

Linden Allee was not designed in this way, nor was it designed for this purpose. It was a row of trees that connected a bridge with an entrance to a forest, and was thus limited by existing conditions in the old city. Just as the Great Elector did not attempt to transform the religious ideas of his subjects, he did not attempt to transform the established routes of the old city. Historians of Berlin, like John Toland, argued that the Great Elector's policy of toleration was represented in the architecture of the city, and the strength of this connection can be tested in an examination of the Elector's building of Berlin's two principal seventeenth- and eighteenth-century suburbs: Dorotheenstadt and Friedrichstadt.

Dorotheenstadt was laid out in 1668 by Memhardt, two years after the death of the Great Elector's wife Louise Henrietta, and the same year as his marriage to Dorothea. In 1674 the new suburb received its civic privileges from the monarch. The compass of Dorotheenstadt was limited on all sides by existing

physical conditions: to the south by Linden Allee, to the north and west by the course of the Spree, and to the east by the newly constructed fortification walls of the old city. The land on which it was built was swampy and had to be drained before the laying of foundations could begin; Memhardt's Dutch training in land reclamation greatly aided this work. The streets of the new suburb formed a grid of oblong blocks, the long sides of which were parallel to Linden Allee and the short sides perpendicular to these. The use of the new buildings on these streets cannot be determined precisely, but a number of probable inferences can be made from what is represented on existing drawings.

In the north-west part of Dorotheenstadt there was a ship-building industry. This was a sensible location in view of the low land, the close proximity of the densely wooded Tiergarten and the river. Presumably the ship-builders lived nearby. La Vigne's plan of 1685 indicates that different kinds of buildings existed at the southern edge of the new development. These are in the form of communal buildings, and were probably occupied by the newly-recruited military forces. During the Great Elector's reign the number of soldiers in his command had increased from 10,000 to 26,000. Further south, on the other side of Linden Allee, La Vigne indicated detached private residences with associated out-buildings for the practice of trades and animal husbandry. However, it is certain that no restrictions were made on the kinds of trades, or the kinds of people that could settle in Dorotheenstadt.

The southern neighbour of Dorotheenstadt, Friedrichstadt, was projected in 1688 by Johann Arnold Nering. Nering was an engineer born in Wesel, but like Memhardt and the Great Elector's other city-builders, he was trained in Holland. Nering took the position of 'Ingenieur-Oberst' in Brandenburg in 1685, seven years after the death of Memhardt and two years after the death of Michael Smids, Memhardt's immediate successor; 1688 was also the year the Great Elector died. Between that year and 1706, the year of Toland's visit to Berlin, Friedrichstadt had been built up as Berlin's largest suburb.

Nering's planning of Friedrichstadt followed the lines of Dorotheenstadt. It, too, consisted of ·oblong blocks on a regular grid. The long sides of the blocks paralleled Linden Allee. And the streets perpendicular to these followed the

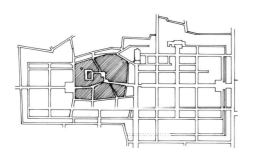

14 Crefeld, examples of Huguenot planning on either side of the Altstadt, after Gutkind.

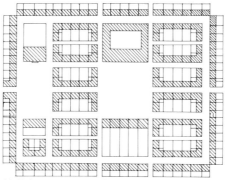

15 Erlangen, a typical gridiron Huguenot development, after Gutkind.

16 Kassel, showing the French settlement outside the fortifications, after Gutkind.

north-south streets of Dorotheenstadt. In fact, the central street of the new development was a continuation of the central street of the older northern suburb. It ran from the northernmost bridge over the Spree across the Linden Allee and the new canal to the bridge over the Floss Graben (a navigable branch of the Spree). From there it continued a short distance to Friedrich's 'Städtler Kirchhof', the city cemetery. This street was named Friedrichstraße. It, like Linden Allee, was not projected into the infinite distance at one end but joined important places in the old city together. Thus, it had nothing whatsoever to do with the formation of a perspective view and its related significance as a representation of individual power. One might say that the power represented there was that of the already existing city.

Another similarity between the two suburbs was that they were both limited in extent by already existing boundaries. To the north of Friedrichstadt was Linden Allee. To the south was the *Floss Graben*. On the east side was Linden Straße, which formed the western limit of Cölnisches Feld, later Köpenicker Vorstadt. The west side of Friedrichstadt was, in fact, the only side which was not limited by a pre-existing boundary.

In general, then, one can observe that the regular block form of the new districts – Dorotheenstadt and Friedrichstadt – was set within an irregular but neither undefined nor ambiguous perimeter. The gridiron plan was reconciled with already constituted places, places with existing significance and contemporary value. This 'style' of laying out urban developments was not, of course, without precedent in the late seventeenth century. Gridiron planning was used in the earlier part of that century by both the Dutch and French, but perhaps the best example of this practice is the planning of the Huguenot towns – Crefeld, Erlangen and the Upper *Neustadt* of Kassel, for example.

Reconsidering Toland's designation of Friedrichstadt as a city of toleration, one recalls that he attributed the 'happy prosperity' of Berlin to the 'liberty of conscience' enjoyed by the Berliners. The city prospered because its citizens feared neither for their lives nor their property. Each citizen patiently tolerated his neighbours no matter how irregular each one's way of life was. The policy of toleration was instituted to 'keep the peace' among people who could not agree with each other. If one accepts the idea that a building is an image or representation of its builder or inhabitants, then according to Toland the policy of toleration was represented architecturally in the lack of stylistic differentiation: because the buildings of Friedrichstadt *tolerated* one another by keeping their distinguishing characteristics from public view, this 'style' reduced civil discord and the aggravation of oppositive sentiments in the city.

This 'style' existed in the plan of the new developments also:

it, too, was undifferentiated. No particular place occupied a privileged position. There was neither a single perspective view built into the form of the streets nor was there a place which put the person who occupied it in competition with others. The gridiron plan worked like the abstract facades to reduce civil discord by neutralisation. Places of distinction were eliminated. No blocks were superior to others, and there was no inherent hierarchy in the layout. The plan regularised connections between existing places of importance, the Tiergarten, the Spree and the city cemetery, and the abstract character of these regularised connections represented a city of toleration.

The Great Elector judged toleration to be the best form of political order. An evaluation of this ranking must now be presented in conclusion. This can be easily accomplished by restating the ideas of toleration in the terms of an old Greek story, the story of Poseidon acting as the 'Earth Shaker'.[11] An outline of this story will enable us to indicate the theoretical shortcomings of the Elector's idea of political order and analogously his city-making. Poseidon is of special interest in this case because his Roman equivalent, Neptune, occupied a privileged position in the Elector's 'Lustgarten'.

The Challenge of Poseidon

In Greek mythology Poseidon is the God of the sea. He was identified by the Romans with their God Neptune, who was probably a late representation of the Etruscan god of lakes and rivers. Another name for the sea god is the Earth Shaker, the one who cleft the mountains with his great trident in order to let his waters pass over the face of the earth. A consequence of this act was that continents of the world became separated: Europe was made distant from Asia and the Aegean Islands were cut off from the mainland. The Earth Shaker effected the primordial division of the world into different lands.

The results of his work of world design can be interpreted as a symbol of the affairs of men. The severance of land from land and island from island is a representation of the severance of people from people and man from man. Poseidon is a symbol of *distance between* things, in Matthew Arnold's words 'the unplumb'd, salt, estranging sea'. The challenge he offers is for reunion, the establishment of common ground or communication between estranged men:

O then a longing like despair
Is to their farthest caverns sent!
For surely once, they feel, we were
Parts of a single continent.
Now round us spreads the watery plain-
O might our marges meet again![12]

In terms of the policy of toleration, the challenge that was offered by Poseidon – represented in Friedrichstadt as Neptune and the Dutch master of the sea – was to accomplish the work of reconciliation, the achievement of public unanimity or *concordia*.

In ancient Greece this challenge was met by Jason, the Navigator. 'In the language of Greek Mythology the Black Sea was transformed from "the inhospitable" into the "hospitable" sea by the heroic enterprise of the Argonauts.'[13] Jason was the one who crossed Poseidon's waters and rejoined those on the Aegean Islands, together with those on the mainland. He accomplished this heroic achievement by charting his course against something just as powerful and unfathomable as Poseidon's waters – but something also constant – the heavens! Jason read the stars, the great and glorious signature of Apollo, the Light revered by sailors of all kinds who find themselves caught in a dark and dangerous sea. Jason met the challenge of Poseidon by deciphering and following what is lasting and permanent, in other words what is essential.

The theoretical shortcomings of the policy of toleration can now be indicated. When seventeenth- and eighteenth-century religious sectarians are compared to the isolated Aegean Islands, and the lack of common sense or *concordia* to the 'unplumb'd salt, estranging sea', then the practice of toleration can be compared to and differentiated from the art of navigation. The navigator accepts the world as it was created by the Gods: there are land masses separated from one another by the dark and inconstant sea. But he is, at the same time, sensitive to man's unhappiness with the divided world, represented by the longing felt by those made distant by the Earth Shaker. The navigator responds to the cry from his fellow men by working toward reconciling them after the essential pattern marked in the heavens. He achieves *concordia* by imitating (in the course he follows) the divine model.

The tolerant man also accepts the world as he finds it: differences of opinion are common among men and many would rather fight than conform to another's beliefs. But the tolerant man does not sense any longing for reunion, nor does he try to interpret what is constant in the world. He accepts isolation as the nature of the human condition and is content when men refrain from persecuting one another. Silence suits toleration very well; where reticence prevails there is no false dominance. But neither is there unanimity. The lack of common sense was a serious problem in late seventeenth-century European cities. It remained so in Berlin, despite the implementation of the policy of toleration.

The Great Elector conceived toleration to be the only alternative to persecution. It should now be clear that there are others. Criminals are neither persecuted nor tolerated: they are punished according to the law. Obviously, there are some things which cannot be tolerated. The representative of the law is intolerant of crime. Just as the navigator says no to any deviation from the right course, the maker of public policy or urban form says no to any offense against the framework of public order. Silence suits the practice of toleration but not the making of cities; the city-maker must be able to say no. And he must be able to say yes! What is public order? What are the essential forms of the city? What is inviolable in urban form? Questions like these are the great and permanently challenging ones. No attempt at any sort of answer is necessary here, merely posing these questions advances the debate beyond the tolerant position and, in fact, hints at the manner in which they must be handled.

Plato wrote that constitutions do not grow on trees but out

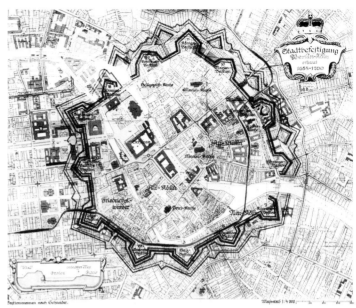

17 Berlin's growth from 1658 to 1700, superimposed onto the 1932 plan. (Ph Landesbildstelle Berlin)

of the souls of men socially dominant in a *polis*. A good city appears when city-makers have had a vision of what is good or essential, and a tolerant city – in contemporary terms, a pluralist city – appears when city-makers have had a vision of what is acceptable. Both visions focus on the world as we live it, there is no difference there. The difference between them simply depends upon what is being searched for, what can be tolerated or what is right.

Notes

1 *The Encyclopedia of Philosophy*, Vol 8, p 143.
2 Eric Voegelin, 'Liberalism and Its History', *The Review of Politics*, No 37, 1974, p 506.
3 *Ibid*, p 505.
4 A Declaration of the Elector of Brandenburg in favour of the French Protestants who shall settle themselves in any of His Dominions, 1686.
5 Adolphus W Ward, 'The Origins of the Kingdom of Prussia', in *The Age of Louis XIV*, Camb Mod Hist, Vol 5, 1908, pp 616-17.
6 John Motley, *The History of the Dutch Republic*, Vol 2, 1889, p 565.
7 Ferdinand Schevill, *The Great Elector*, 1947.
8 Max Osborn, *Berlin*, 1909, p 60.
9 Eberhard Hemple, *Baroque Art and Architecture in Central Europe*, 1965, p 74.
10 Marie Gothein, *History of Garden Art*, Vol 2, p 46.
11 Arnold Toynbee, *A Study of History*, Vol 1, 1945, pp 325-27.
12 Matthew Arnold, *Isolation*, quoted in Toynbee, *ibid*, p 326.
13 *Ibid*, p 327.

Sources

E Berner, *Geschichte des Preuss. Stades*, 1891.
W Boeck, *Alte Gartenkunst*, 1939.
Albert Geyer, *Geschichte des Schlosses zu Berlin*, 1936.
F A Kuntze, *Das Alte Berlin*, 1937.
O Teichert, *Ziergarten und die Ziergartenerei*, 1865.
Hennebo-Hoffman, *Geschichte Der Deutschen Gartenkunst*.
Werner Hegemann *Das Steinerne Berlin*, Berlin 1930.
Hans Muther, *Berlin's Bautradition*, Berlin.

David Leatherbarrow
Born in the USA. Studied architecture at the University of Kentucky, and worked in architecture and city-planning offices after graduation. In 1976 came to England on a Fulbright Scholarship to study the history and theory of architecture at the University of Essex. Is finishing a PhD thesis on eighteenth-century architecture and gardens. Is a founder-member of the Association for Metropolitan Arts and teaches architectural history and design at the Polytechnic of Central London.

1 Schinkel, Friedrich-Werdersche Kirche, Gothic project.

Julius Posener
Schinkel's Eclecticism and 'the Architectural'

The 'Schinkelfest' is one of the finest traditions which the architectural profession has maintained: in Berlin it is *the* finest. In March the members of the profession meet to honour the memory of the architect who was of paramount importance for Berlin. The question is not whether he was the greatest: one has to grow old to find that he was. In the course of my life there have been developments in Berlin architecture which appeared more interesting. Beside these architects Schinkel may on occasions have appeared a little pale and antiquated; but if we look at their effect on Berlin, even that of Mendelsohn, who has erected an impressive number of major buildings here, or Bruno Taut, who gave whole residential areas an individual profile: their work seems one-sided compared with Schinkel's. Schinkel was universal. He was universal because, as royal architect and private architect for members of the Royal family, he built everything: public buildings, barracks, bridges, country seats and even what the British call 'follies'. He was universal in another sense as well: he built in every possible form. That is something I shall be talking about later.

In Berlin the spatial encounter with Schinkel was, one could almost say, inevitable. It no longer is, at any rate, for us here in the West. Not only because we only rarely have an opportunity to see the Schinkel country in the city centre, the 'Neue Wache', the 'Altes Museum', the residence of the Prussian Prince-Successor, the Friedrich Werder church: Potsdam is closed to us as well. Of Schinkel's Potsdam we only have the outer edges, Schloss Glienicke, the buildings in the park and the follies on the Pfaueninsel, but we do not have Babelsberg or Charlottenhof. But when I was a child, Schinkel's realm was so big that it was really impossible to avoid him. In the museums, the churches, palaces, schools, barracks of the first half, indeed the first two-thirds of the last century, his influence was manifest, even when the buildings were not his but those of his contemporaries and followers. Schinkel stopped work in 1841, but that was not the end of his influence which was felt by others: Persius, Stueler and architects whose names are largely forgotten.

I have a confession to make: this ever-constant presence of Schinkel and his influence could be oppressive. As a young man I hated Schinkel. It was enough to hear Goethe as an old man talk about him as 'the excellent Schinkel', never forgetting to mention the exalted position he held, to arouse a feeling of defiance in me. I never imagined then that I would be invited to speak to you here today, ladies and gentlemen, on an occasion like this. Schinkel to me was a figure like Spohr or Hummel in music. They were 'excellent masters' too, and like Schinkel concerned to compensate for the loss of *tradition*, which ended in Germany with the strange forms of the rococo, with the smoothness of a *convention*, diluting the past in sugar water in order to use it again. And indeed the Gothic of the Friedrich Werder church appeared no less sugary to me than the acanthus decorations on the Hundebrücke – as it was first called. Well, one could make allowances for that, and why should one hate it so much, even at an immature age?

But there was something fatal about the influence of the established artists and administrators of that period, the years, say, between 1820 and 1850. They had found a formula; it might be difficult to define, but they took some pains to see that it was accepted. It was not easy to grasp, because the distinction between classicism and romanticism, as Goethe had established it, when he spoke of classicism as the healthy element and romanticism as the unhealthy, was no longer valid. That was easy enough to grasp, and Goethe could have taken Schinkel the Hellenist as the crown witness for classicism. But that would have been to misunderstand him, as later on he was misunderstood; Schinkel may have preferred the architecture of the ancients but he did not consider himself bound to it; he never regarded it as the only possibility for his own century. Goethe, by the way, also became more catholic in his taste: after the 'Divan' and Boisserée had aroused his interest in the building of the Cologne cathedral, Goethe, too, extended the values he considered fitting. When he visited Italy in 1786, the rebirth of antiquity in the works of Raphael conquered his medievalism; it was something like a change of government in Goethe's spiritual realm. The objects which he had venerated in his youth were no longer admitted. But now, when von Hammer and his friend Sulpice opened his eyes to whole provinces of human creation – antiquity receded into the background for a time: the realm of that which was acceptable was extended. The question was, then, what valid criteria remained after all the borders had become fluid. 'Classicism is healthy, romanticism is unhealthy': that was clear. But now more general values had to be adduced. If so much was admitted that formerly had been excluded, how could the romantics, against whom the feud was still being conducted even if in a much milder form, be kept at bay? He admired the same objects as they did, he even cooperated with Boisserée, the arch-romantic.

The answer was to fall back on a higher – if you like –concept of validity. You might call it a less clear, a vaguer concept, for what it ultimately amounted to was a personal censorship. 'I decide,' said Göring, 'who is a Jew'. And Goethe during the last two decades of his life could have said: 'I decide what is valid.' For all the breadth of research on Goethe, the limits of what was acceptable in his domain have never been, so far as I can see, clearly defined. *Which* Gothic buildings, for instance, were acceptable? Altenberg certainly, he calls it perfect. But would he have accepted the cathedral in Schwerin? Or the late Gothic halls in the castles in Prague and Meissen? We do not know. We neither know the full extent of what he was acquainted with at the end of his life – it must have been considerable; nor do we know what ultimately he did reject. From the pronouncements of the last years there emanates a feeling of good will which seems boundless; but there obviously *were* limits and they were strictly observed. We can judge by the language of the last years, an official language, in which he speaks of 'gratifying activity', 'inestimable' drawings which

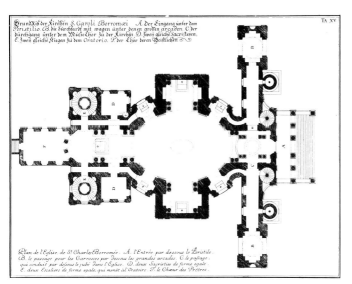

2 J.B. Fischer von Erlach, Carlskirche plan, *Entwurff Einer Historischer Architectur.*

3 Carlskirche elevation.

Schinkel has 'acquired' on a journey and of a certain propriety, which although it does not exclude boldness and depth, increasingly tends to allow them only to one person: Goethe.

If I am not mistaken, there is a very comparable spirit in Schinkel's work. The stylistic possibilities of his work were almost unlimited, and the two canonical possibilities, Greek and Gothic, did not remain the only ones. Romanesque, Byzantine, Egyptian, and Renaissance decorations were used, and not only on his stage sets. There were also the possibilities offered by the new techniques which were emerging and which Schinkel made use of: smooth brick buildings, which can almost be called timeless, like the Arcona lighthouse, even iron bridges. The realm becomes so great that the 'Schinkelfeste', one of which has brought us together today, are very welcome, indeed they are very necessary; the great complex which makes up Schinkel's work can, should and ought to be re-interpreted again and again. Six months ago the German Architects' Association gave its major award to Mies van der Rohe and naturally Schinkel was mentioned: Schinkel, who was admired by Mies, and Mies may be called a follower of Schinkel. That sequence is generally accepted now: Schinkel – Behrens – Mies. But a few years ago our greatly honoured Heinrich Lauterbach stood here and gave a wonderful talk in which he called Schinkel the predecessor of Hugo Häring, Häring, whose views had been strongly opposed to those of Mies.

Schinkel's work is open to very different interpretations: and these differences in interpretation can be justified. That is why we maintain our tradition of meeting to honour his name. But though his work is many-sided, it embodies certain values. Like Goethe, Schinkel kept an open mind, admitting many possibilities. Like Goethe, he was nevertheless a severe judge: for Schinkel, too, propriety is a condition of that which is acceptable. The architect is at an advantage here. His values are more definite. He can replace vague concepts such as excellence with a more tangible quality. Let us call this quality the *architectural.*

This new concept only applies after about 1800. It becomes significant at the moment when tradition comes to an end, for it is only then that it is necessary. It is the correlative of eclecticism, or it would be better to say that eclecticism is *its* correlative. Let me talk about eclecticism for a moment. I think it is something which is frequently misunderstood. And if I say that

after 1800 eclecticism was the correlative of the architectural I owe you an explanation.

Schinkel was an eclectic, but he did not invent eclecticism. Eclecticism is older than is generally supposed. Can we say that it goes back to the beginning of the Renaissance? We can ignore Ancient Roman eclecticism in this context. Does Western eclecticism begin with the Renaissance? I do not think so. The return to one particular style of the past is not eclecticism, although we may call the Renaissance a first step towards eclecticism. But Fischer von Erlach may perhaps be called an eclectic; he published his great historical work in 1723, the first history of architecture, in which not only the architecture of Egypt, Greece and Rome is discussed, but also Gothic buildings and Turkish, Persian, Indian, Chinese and Japanese architecture, as far as they were known at that time. And they were much better known than we imagine.

In his introduction Fischer says that his collection is meant for pleasure and 'to stimulate the artists.' If we look at his own work – one of his major creations like the 'Karl Borromaeus' church in Vienna – we see that he certainly allowed himself to be stimulated. With such an erudite architect we cannot say that it is coincidence that there are two Trajan columns before the church or that these columns are really minarets (I mean that they stand in the position minarets would have occupied in a Persian cupola mosque). The plan of the church corresponds to one of these mosques except that a retrochoir has been added which resembles the one in Andrea Palladio's church 'Il Redentore' in Venice. Fischer knew Palladio's church well. So here we notice a number of quotations and adaptations. Probably Fischer's contemporaries only recognised – and, I assume – approved of the quotations: the Trajan columns and perhaps the retrochoir. To recognise the adaptations, the features derived from the mosque, one would have needed to be as erudite as the author of the plan. We can take it that he smiled to himself and kept them secret, like contemporary composers who added figures to their scores which had only graphic or symbolic meaning and were not audible.

The style of the church in Vienna, which is pure Baroque, absorbs all the borrowed elements into one great work, just as Fischer's history is baroque and presents the art of the Greeks, the Persians and all the others in a baroque manner. Fischer's eclecticism is not yet what we understand by the word. Nevertheless, it constitutes an essential step towards eclecticism, because Fischer takes seriously the products of strange and exotic architectures. They are no longer, as they had been up to then, disregarded as the work of barbarians. However, as long as the style of the period, let us say eighteenth-century Baroque, remains binding, foreign elements can be absorbed in it, as the pagodas and Chinese tea-houses of the Rococo clearly show. Even Vanbrugh Castle near Greenwich, the home of an eccentric architect and the first essay, perhaps of a Gothic revival, has an entrance which dates it unmistakably: it clearly belongs to the beginning of the eighteenth century. Indeed, one has to go to England to find the first signs of a movement which can almost be called eclecticism: I mean the Gothic revival and a little later the Greek revival. Strawberry Hill in Twickenham, Horace Walpole's Gothic country seat and the Greek orders, which in fashionable architecture followed so quickly on the work of Stewart and Revett on the Acropolis, belong in the 1760s. Until then only the Roman orders were known because the Renaissance had used them and not the Greek orders. Even these two revivals, however, cannot be called eclecticism: there was a fairly strict limitation to Greek and Gothic. It was after 1800 that this limitation fell. One only needs to think of Brighton Pavilion, built by Nash for the Regent in the Indian style.

A certain relaxation had begun in England, a readiness to play with any form as long as it was pleasing to the eye. The charming effects which could be achieved with this elegant relaxation were well known to Schinkel, certainly after 1826, the year of his visit to England. These charming pieces still belonged in a way to the general style of the time: they hardly stood out. They were more or less part of the Regency style. English eclecticism was a gradual move into a state in which there would no longer be a binding architecture, a long process of dissolution whose products would still keep to the Regency rules until about 1840. Look at the Tudor dress of Pugin's Parliament buildings: they are still as much Regency Gothic as the pagodas and tea-houses of the eighteenth century were genuine *dix-huitième*. But look at Pugin's churches, buildings in which he expressed his real artistic and moral aims: they are quite different. What differentiates them from Regency – and from Pugin's own Regency Gothic – is their uncompromising *ugliness*. They are the first buildings to be on the other side of a tradition which in England knows no Rococo and which continues from the Renaissance with a series of variations on classical architecture until it finally comes to an end with Regency itself.

On the continent, especially in Germany, there is no architecture to correspond to Regency. At most the Rue de Rivoli might be called a French version; at most, I say. But German Neoclassicism has nothing metropolitan about it. It was both more restricted and less modern than Regency architecture, and less binding. Goethe's 'Gartenhaus' achieves the freedom which was apparent everywhere in England, but that was a garden house. The new bourgeois form, which is still affecting a kind of Neoclassicism, though only just, is on the continent, and especially in Germany, only apparent in interiors, in the 'Biedermeier'. Perhaps it is no coincidence that Schinkel's furniture appeals immediately even to those who have little real taste for his architecture; at any rate some of his furniture, his light, straightforward, well-constructed chairs, tables and cupboards, especially the chairs. They are his real contribution to the 'Biedermeier.'

As the tradition came to an end earlier on the continent, and very much earlier in Germany, eclecticism here is rather different from that in England. It is certainly not a relaxed and elegant drift into a final dissolution, it is a very serious affair. Before beginning this discourse on eclecticism we called it the correlative of the architectural. It is preceded by that very promising but ephemeral move to a new architecture with which the names of Boullée and Ledoux are connected, artists after all, from the last third of the eighteenth century. Schinkel was indebted to this architecture through his teacher Gilly. The Paris influence is very clear in one of the works of his youth, the design for the stairs for Schloss Köstritz of 1803, and was still evident in the 'Neue Wache' of 1816. But the revolutionary architecture did not hold Schinkel for long, and it is idle to speculate whether things would have been different had Gilly lived longer. He did *not* live longer and although in his construction sketches he anticipated things to come much later, Friedrich Gilly was the last of a line, indeed one could almost say he was a latecomer. He was the last and perhaps the greatest master of the architecture of the French Revolution. One could perhaps speculate on whether Friedrich Gilly would have moved away from this style himself had he been able to go on working. He might – one could say this is a real possibility –have become another Schinkel.

For the architecture of the Revolution, like the Revolution itself, was a miscarriage – that is, its indirect and more lasting results were quite different, of quite a different style, from what their creators intended, whether their names were Boullée and Ledoux or St Just. The true heir and systematician of the movement was Durand. Durand was a pupil of Boullée and lectured in architecture at Napoleon's École Polytechnique. The essentials of what he taught between 1802 and 1805 are in his book *Précis des Leçons Données à l'École Polytechnique*. By then Durand was no longer unknown, for the book that had become known as 'Durand's Heavy Volume' had appeared in 1800, his *Receuil et Parallèle des Édifices en Tout Genre, Anciens et Modernes*, a collection of historical and more recent examples of every kind of building. It contains Egyptian, Greek and especially Roman architecture, but it also includes Renaissance architecture and even some examples of Gothic, although not very many. There are even mosques and pagodas. This is not, like Fischer von Erlach's work, an historical treatise in an easily accessible style, intended to delight the eyes and stimulate; it is really a text-book. Precisely for that reason it is interesting to see Gothic and Islamic architecture here beside the antique. The *Précis* draws the necessary conclusions. Even in the *Receuil* there are very isolated value judgements. The *Précis* consistently pursues the aim of replacing traditional architecture with one more suited to the purposes of the bourgeois state. The first page of the book is significant: it introduces the Panthéon in Paris, Soufflot's construction of 1757, and comments: *'Église Ste Geneviève ou Panthéon Français, tel qu'il est – Cet édifice quoiqu'assez resserré a côuté dix-huit millions.'* ('St. Geneviève's Church or the French Panthéon as it is; this rather cramped building cost eighteen million.')

Beside it is Durand's own proposal for a Panthéon which, by the way, looks very like the Roman Pantheon, with the following comment: *'Le Panthéon Français, tel qu'on auroit dû le faire – n'en eut côuté que neuf et eut été vaste et magnifique.'* ('The French Pavilion as one would have done it, costing half; it would have been vast and magnificent.') This is followed by pages elucidating the constructions and plan elements of an *architecture civique*. The emphasis is on simplicity: the constructions are elementary and the plan elements grow from the smallest to ever larger units, all drawn on paper, divided into little squares and always repeating the same prescribed solutions until finally the museum, the university, the hospital and the prison, in short all the buildings the bourgeois state

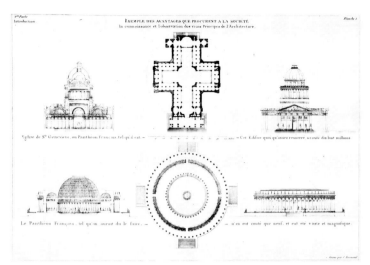

4 J.-N.-L. Durand, Panthéon ('*tel qu'il est*'), *Précis des Leçons d'Architecture* 1805.

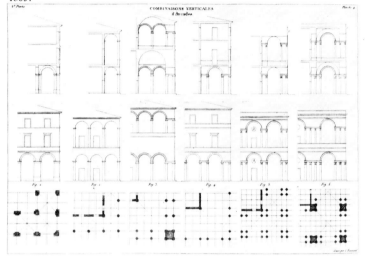

5 Durand, Combinaison verticales, same source.

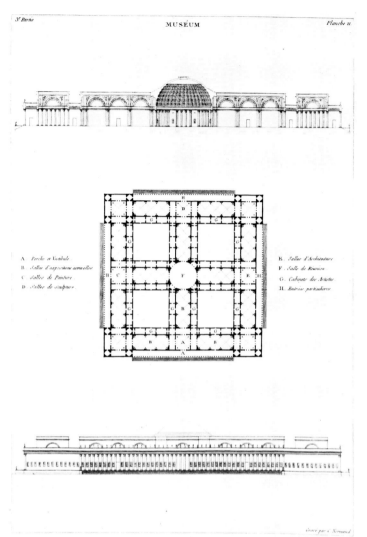

6 Durand, Museum (or library) plan.

required, emerge in typical form.

Even the *Receuil* contained buildings which Antiquity had not known. These are generally interpretations of Antiquity by Palladio or Vignola, masters who were accepted for they were not caught in the bad tradition. 'Palladio's farm-houses', says the text which Legrand, Durand's friend and ally, composed for him, 'with their tiled or thatched roofs, are worth very much more than Borromini's extravagant palaces or Guarino Guarini's rich and bizarre creations'. In the *Précis* Durand's typical public buildings are stylistically close to Ancient Rome, while smaller and lighter buildings, garden houses, for example, terraces and flights of steps are reminiscent of the Italian villa, whose pleasing architecture does not seem to belong to any particular style. It is specifically demonstrated that style is anyway losing its importance: columns and pilasters may still be applied, but the load-bearing wall may do without them and round or even pointed arches may be used. In fact, any forms may be selected to express the same thing, say a load-bearing wall with windows, and so we see that form is no longer what *matters*.

Schinkel will no doubt have known this book. If he did not own it – and that could be established, no doubt – he would certainly have seen it. It is hardly conceivable that any architect of standing at the time could have overlooked it. A man in Schinkel's position could not afford to overlook it, entrusted as he was with the task of creating an *architecture civique* for the Prussian state. And there are drawings in Durand's book which look like studies for the Pantheon hall in the 'Altes Museum' and others which look like studies for the 'casino' near Schloss Glienicke. But we should not put too much significance on this, for forms like these were current throughout Europe at the time; very certainly we cannot say that Schinkel simply *carried out* Durand's ideas.

There are two things in particular which mark Schinkel off from Durand: firstly, the smaller scale of state architecture in Prussia, which was a great advantage. The Prussian stage on which Durand moved was smaller than the world stage without being in any way provincial. No-one will deny that Schinkel's creations were regarded by his contemporaries, and not only the Prussians, as being in the very forefront of their time. He may in fact have inherited this modernity from Durand, but he was spared having to erect the huge soulless machines which fill Durand's book. Instead of a huge museum he could build the 'Altes Museum', a building of ideal proportions. A similar Durand-Schinkel relation can be seen in Schinkel's other works.

The second difference is in Schinkel's freer and richer eclecticism, although Schinkel's preferences were clearly where Durand had found his models, in Antiquity; yet stylistically Schinkel was very much less restricted than Durand. That is certainly in part due to his knowledge of England, where these things were taken more lightly and more imaginatively. It is not up to me to point to a third difference and say that Schinkel was a genius and Durand's mind was a junk-shop.

Nevertheless, the junk-shop proved of immense value to the genius. For Durand's work justifies eclecticism as a correlative – and a necessary correlative – to the concept of the architectural.

We have just seen that Durand was not concerned with individual forms. The École des Beaux-Arts followed him in this view right into our century. The historical styles could be used simply because they were no longer taken seriously and it was no more than a mild Neoclassicism, a tame reflection of the revolutionary Neoclassicism of a man like Boullée, which determined the general attitude of Durand to antiquity. The eclecticism of a Durand – and of a Schinkel – is not (as the Greek and Gothic revivals still were) born of enthusiasm for a specific form from the past. Even their enthusiasm for Antiquity is moderate. Durand uses it as a model because it was the only established architecture of imperial dimensions: the only historical *architecture civique* whose function could be compared with the functions Durand's buildings had to fulfil. The style itself called forth at most a mild enthusiasm. The new, the real, eclecticism as it appears for the first time in Durand's work, is on the contrary based on the interchangeability of all historical styles. They were admissible because they had to serve a new concept, the architectural.

It is high time we discussed this concept. When I was a schoolboy our German master once commented: 'If we Prussians were Buddhists we would have made Buddhism a thoroughly proper affair'. Schinkel can let his buildings be Buddhist *à la rigeur*, but certainly medieval and religious, Florentine and princely – they could even be Swiss alpine –provided they *behaved in a proper manner*. Anything was admissible as long as a Schinkel presented it in an orderly fashion. But the architectural is more than a code of behaviour. For the first time a major principle appears, and Auguste Perret still firmly believed in it: the doctrine of the 'eternal laws' which constitute the architectural. In fact: if the Gothic church was planned according to the same principles as the Renaissance palace, the Egyptian temple or the Roman colonnade, the stylistic forms did not matter, they were of only secondary importance.

In Schinkel's day the attempt was not made to formulate those eternal laws on which the architecture of all times was based. Durand at most indicates that it rests on order: on the little squares he used. Later on Guadet, the theoretician of the École des Beaux-Arts, did formulate those laws. Howard Robertson's book on 1923 – as late as that! – is a version from our own time. After his *Principles of Architectural Design* Robertson produced a second book, *Principles of Modern Design*. From his point of view that was consistent: for if all architects follow the same eternal laws the latest architecture must do so, too, or it cannot be regarded as architecture. So he forces Dudok, Mendelsohn and Le Corbusier into a canon which was totally alien to these masters, even Le Corbusier. Indeed we can say that Robertson's second book did much to weaken his first, for it then became fully apparent what nonsense there is behind titles such as composition, balance, unity, dominant, variation, etc. The time of Durand and Schinkel was wise to avoid any definite statement. The architectural may be *eo ipso* a more generally valid criterion than Goethe's very personal criteria had been but Schinkel, too, was really saying: 'I decide who is a Jew'; in other words, I decide what is architectural. He might actually have said: 'I am the one who creates it.'

But it would never have occurred to him to say that. There may not have been a definition of the architectural in Schinkel's day but there was a clear consensus on what should be understood by it. We have seen how great the influence of Durand's book was. And if Schinkel's realm was incomparably wider than Durand's, if it contained reminiscences of the architecture of the French Revolution, experiences of the eclectic practice of the English architects and a modern pragmatism to which we owe his 'timeless' works, it was all assimilated and it could only be assimilated because the binding law, the architectural, was always present in the architect's mind even if it was never enunciated.

Today we know that this concept of the architectural was based on an error. We know that there are no eternal laws, that it is not true that the Egyptians, for instance, and the Gothic architects worked to the same laws. It may be true that they both worked geometrically but the geometries they used were

7 K.F. Schinkel, Altes Museum, plan.

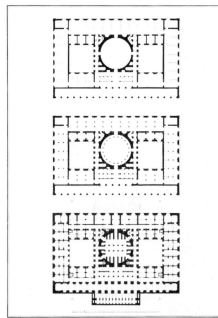

8 Schinkel, Altes Museum, elevation.

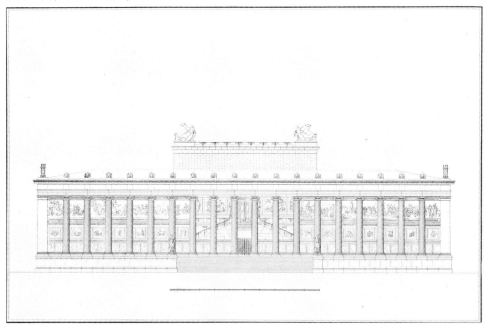

9 Schinkel, Friedrich-Werdersche Kirche, Byzantine project.

the Florentine house-fronts in Berlin. It was artificial, an architect's architecture, and one for the educated classes. Muthesius said of this Neoclassical architecture: 'While the crafts, the essential basis of all artistic achievement, were dying slowly from starvation and persecution, our educated classes still went on raving about something they believed to be higher and purer in art, the ultimate harmonic unity of a world art which they imputed to the concept of Greek classicism. It was mainly apparent in that it floated like a phantom in the air, hardly touching the ground of life. No doubt that was why the age was known as the age of idealism.' That is spiteful, and we would do well to see it in the context of Muthesius's own period and his particular purpose. But ultimately the designation 'in the air' can hardly be surprising; after all I have just said that Schinkel created an architecture in a vacuum: the air, a vacuum, that is the historical place of this architecture. The architectural: a new concept, which was never formulated, let alone defined; it was only known – I want to avoid the word 'felt'. It was something stronger and clearer than a feeling: the architectural, unconsciously known, made it possible for Schinkel's work to emerge in a vacuum and maintain itself in a vacuum.

That is something which matters to us.

Some of you may be inclined to support me in this. Words like 'the architectural' sound well in an architect's ears. But please do not forget that this concept of the architectural is not much more than my own working hypothesis. I shall have to substantiate this. It was not entirely without reason that I asked you to follow me in my examination of the genesis of this concept in Schinkel's age. What we saw was this: the concept of the architectural appeared when tradition had ceased. It provided a standard for new tasks and new dimensions. It appeared in the aftermath of a revolution. It was valid in an architecture which was designed for everyone. Durand was certainly right when he looked back at Roman Hellenism as the only period comparable with his own. The prevailing conditions were similar. Roman Hellenism also created a civic architecture of new dimensions; it, too, had new tasks to solve and solved them objectively, by subordinating them to a severe and often schematic order and giving them a generally binding appearance.

Two years ago Heinrich Lauterbach on this occasion discussed the amphitheatre in Verona and read out to us the entry in Goethe's diary of his journey to Italy where he speaks of the crater which the antique architect created, as simply as possible, through art. That is one side of the Roman practice. It took whatever task it had to perform seriously and performed it objectively as in this case it let human activity solidify, so to speak, into a building. You see the other side when you go down and look at the remains of the outer ring, a thoroughly well-built piece of Roman Hellenist architecture, whose *dignitas romana* reduces the surrounding buildings – and there are some imposing ones here – to triviality. In those days the architectural, what was binding, was held to lie in columns and entablature. Only purely utilitarian buildings were free of them.

In Schinkel's time, however, what was binding was merely an attitude. Schinkel did not insist on columns and entablature although he liked to use them, and although he always insisted on an architecture, he conferred dignity even upon utilitarian buildings through the architectural arrangement of some period of the past. The grand dignity of Roman architecture could no longer apply in Schinkel's bourgeois age and the rigidly binding attitude, which gave buildings the same columns and

different. In other words, we can prove that the Berlin contractor in the well-known joke was really wrong when he said to his client: 'The house is finished in the rough. Which style do you want me to put on it?' – although it is almost in keeping with the Schinkel attitude: he made projects in different styles for almost every one of his major buildings thinking that the same church, for instance, could be planned in the Gothic, the Byzantine and the Renaissance style. We consider this an error, but this error is part of Schinkel's concept of the architectural, the concept to which he subordinated his life's work. And what a life's work it was!

The concept of the architectural was necessary and its correlative, eclecticism, was equally necessary, for a tradition, a sequence of styles acknowledged by everyone, no longer existed. In Germany there was not even a Regency architecture, which might be termed a gentle bourgeois last word of traditional architecture. Germany had no Regency architecture, only a kind of Regency interior decoration. At that point, Schinkel's work provided a standard in the architectural which was beyond tradition. For a young man in the Twenties of our century it might have seemed as if he had poured sugar water over all the traditions. *Of course* Schinkel thoroughly misunderstood every tradition: to misunderstand them was the prerequisite of his achievement. But his achievement was that through the sheer volume of his work – and we have seen that it was continued after his death – and through its total commitment to the architectural, Schinkel and his followers, but Schinkel himself especially, succeeded in creating an architecture in a vacuum.

It is an architecture without roots, anti-traditional and ephemeral, for when its time was passed, chaos broke loose, although a reflection of its architectural quality is still visible in entablature whatever their purpose, was at least softened. Schinkel's concept of the architectural remained, however, a framework, which maintains life and elevates it; which serves life, without subordinating itself to it. Schinkel represented the independence of architecture from daily life and its intensification of life in the figures which enliven his drawings. People like this have never existed. They move in an idealistic world, Schinkel's world of the architectural.

Compare them with the robust figures in Le Corbusier's drawings!

Certainly we will not be able to follow Schinkel so far. We cannot try to train life along the framework of our architecture as if it were a trellis for training fruit trees. We are nearer to Le Corbusier's figures, although they too suggest a certain idealism, that is, a touch of the unreal.

But if the attitude of our age, a third age of public architecture, an architecture for everybody and an architecture of hitherto unknown dimensions, if our attitude can no longer be that of the concept of the architectural created for Schinkel, that does not mean that we must do without any similar concept altogether. I have just used a formulation for Schinkel's architecture and would like to repeat it: his architecture served life without subordinating itself to it. But that does not only apply to *his* architecture. If I am not mistaken, every architecture does that – or it ought to do so. It is in this remnant of independence and intrinsic value of what is built that I locate the architectural. For we are wrong if we assume that a building – or any object – serves us and that that is all of its reality. We build a house for ourselves and adjust it to suit our needs and desires. But as soon as it is finished, as soon as it has become reality, we have to live with it and we have to adjust ourselves to it. There is nothing which we own on earth to which we ourselves do not in turn belong. And as this is so, ladies and gentlemen, as nothing which we create for our own use subordinates itself completely to this purpose – and to us – I believe that this remainder, this small area of autonomy which remains, is the field in which the architect may work. But in saying this I do not mean that the architect can create art out of this: visual art. Visual art has always constituted the greatest temptation to the architect. This is not the place to discuss at what periods visual art may have been the natural, legitimate expression of the architect. But I doubt that it can be today. Nor do I mean that the architect can use that freedom which remains to him like a lever to alienate the appearance of the building from its purpose so that it ultimately appears to the observer as something quite different from what it is. A grandiose example of that is the opera house in Sydney. A critic has called it 'autonomy of expression'. But where a structure only expresses itself, where the augurs are in agreement, as they are here, for instance, and the theatres in this opera house are not essential to it, we may ask what after all is being expressed here. I am of the opinion, on the contrary, that it is the purpose which a building serves and the means it uses to do so, which create expression in architecture. You may call this the art in architecture. But this art is something different from visual art.

The self-expression of a building is architectural when it is clear beyond doubt, and convincing. For an architect is not expressing his own happiness and sorrow, like a poet, for instance. Planning is not an individual activity, it is work for the community as a whole. There may be buildings, of course there are, which are unmistakably formed by the mind of one man. But they are not a *personal* expression in the way that a poem is. The requirement for the architect to deny direct expression to his own person is probably the hardest he is faced

10 Schinkel, Friedrich-Werdersche Kirche, perspective.

with. Schinkel, a master, whose person is always recognisable in his buildings, still met that requirement.

The element of the architectural is what is general, not individual. It is in that sense that it matters to us, as an attitude. Since those faraway days of Roman Hellenism it has come nearer to its real existence in the everyday aspect of every building. In Schinkel it is still aiming to elevate life. Architecture has since given up that pedagogic intent. One could say that now the opposite is true: architecture takes its sovereignty from everyday life. It has become epic. In the epos, everyday life sees itself as significant. Architecture is no longer aiming to elevate life; nor is it inclined to subject itself to it blindly. It serves the living day, if I may borrow that Goethean phrase, from which it receives its light; it gives in return service, meaning and permanence.

Translated from the German by Eileen Martin.

Julius Posener
Born in 1904 in Berlin. Studied architecture under Hans Poelzig and between 1929 and 1933 he was an assitant to Charles Siclis and André Lurcat in Paris and with Eric Mendelsohn in Berlin. Left Germany in 1933. In 1935 he worked with L'Architecture d'Aujourd'hui, *Boulogne-sur-Seine. Subsequently was assistant to Eric Meldelsohn in Jerusalem. Architect for the President of the Lebanese Republic in Beirut. Editor of the magazine* Hayinyan *(The Builder) in Tel-Aviv. Worked for the Department of Public Works during the Palestine Mandate. In 1941-47 was a British Army volunteer. In 1956 built the Brixton School of Building, London, and began to write on architecture. From 1956-61 was Head of the Department of Architectue at the Technical College in Kuala Lumpur, Malaysia. In 1961 was Professor of History, Theory and Architectural Criticism at the Hochschule für Bildende Kunste. In 1971 was the Emeritus Professor at the Technische Universitat, Berlin. Is a fellow of the Berlin Akademie der Kunste and the Deutsches Werkbund of which he was president from 1972-76. Has been regularly involved in direct political action on many fronts.*

Note:
This article is a revision to an address given at the 112th Schinkelfest in Berlin in 1967.

Goerd Peschken and Tilmann Heinisch
Berlin at the Beginning of the Twentieth Century

Berlin at the beginning of our century – it was still standing when one studied architecture there in 1953. Even the Berlin of the 'Gründerzeit' was still visible as a shell: in the city, one could see facade after facade prickly with decoration and elaborate gables with wrought-iron flag-poles bizarrely silhouetted against the sky. The shops and offices from around the turn of the century were not burnt down, only disfigured; the iron framework of the roofs was often visible, empty and twisted against the light, the surfaces of sculptured cornices and skeleton pillars having spalled off in fires or having been fragmented by bombs and machine-gun fire. All these skeleton buildings might still be standing had there been no need to make room for the compulsively oversize buildings of the East-West competition: buildings neither side is particularly proud of now.

Before the First World War the former city had stretched unbroken from Alexander Platz to Potsdamer Strasse and had only moved west to Wittenbergplatz in isolated areas. The city with its shops and offices was most dense around the old medieval town: Haackescher Markt, Wallstrasse, Spittelmarkt, Hausvogteiplatz; it then grew and broadly followed the suburbs of the Absolutist period through Friedrichstadt and along Leipziger Strasse to Potsdamer Platz. The 'Prussian cap', a roof design consisting of bricks between iron supports, had long been a familiar feature. In many of the older business premises, only the downstairs (or at most, the two lower storeys) had solid frame ceilings, so that when Berlin burned the falling beams burst through these caps. The type of building with business premises in all five storeys was only introduced in Berlin around 1885-90, at first with premises rented to individual enterprises. The big companies which developed the department store adopted the skeleton type after some hesitation around 1895, and this was followed by the breathtaking development of the department store which found its architectural peak in Messel's Wertheim building on

Leipziger Platz. Messel, who had played a part in the development of the Berlin department store right from the beginning, had produced a very stark version for the older front of the Wertheim building on Leipziger Strasse in 1896-7; it consisted of little more than pillars and glass. The famous building of 1904 on Leipziger Platz, visible from afar and in a unique site forming part of the entrance to the city centre, was not modest but was extremely elegant and quite unforgettable for anyone who saw it. Everyone I have heard speak of the interior describes the experience as similar to that in a Gothic cathedral: a sensation of size, sublimity and costliness in every detail and an intense atmosphere.

In 1896, in *Berlin und seine Bauten*, Otto March comments that stimulus from England and America was evident in the shops and office buildings, both countries being far ahead of Germany in trade. But in the following years the German economy caught up so quickly that by the turn of the century the monopolisation of the retail trade had produced its own type of building as it had its own type of business; March, we may add, played a considerable part in this.

The most striking feature of architectural development in Berlin after 1900 is the emergence of elegance and good taste. The extraordinary success of Messel's highly sensitive and delicate building is due in no small part to this. The trend seems more obvious in Berlin (and Germany) than in neighbouring countries because the works of the preceding generation were particularly ugly here. It seems as if the cultivated German Liberals, whose back Bismarck had broken with the huge success of his power policy between 1866 and 1871, had simply gone under in the stream of *nouveau richesse* which swept over the exploding city of Berlin. No amount of nostalgia can wipe away the impression of heaviness and vulgarity which the Berlin of the 1880s made. It has gone now; there are only a few traces left in the suburbs, but the coldness and lack of perception with which historical material was used remain.

1 Leipziger Strasse looking east before the 1939-45 war. Messel's Wertheim Department Store is at left centre.

2 The Leipziger Platz facade of Messel's Wertheim Department Store, 1904 (second phase): 'extremely elegant and quite unforgettable.'

Messel's Wertheim building was historical, too: on the exterior a virtuoso 'Jugendstil' mixture of mainly late Gothic impulses with a Baroque mansard roof. Aesthetically, however, it had the same effect as the roofs in the English country house style, and in the interior Neoclassical and 'Jugendstil' elements coincided. However, every form was imbued with a spirit –'durchseelt' – to use a contemporary expression. Of course, this was the refinement of taste of a second generation; but it is striking that of all things, the new monopolisation of the retail trade was given such sublimation. The main building of the Wertheim store ennobled, one might say, the whole shopping area of the city to which it formed the entrance and struck the major chord.

In the quieter part of the city centre, the new building of the 'Staatsbibliothek' was *the* event of the years between 1905 and 1910. In the office of the court architect Ernst v. Ihne, the facades had been designed in the most elegant, tasteful Neo-Baroque. Anyone who goes round the whole building (which occupies an entire block) and looks at it carefully will see traits of Berlin Neoclassicism in the side streets; anyone who looks into the lightwells with the white-glazed tiles will find pure 'Jugendstil' Neoclassicism rather in the Viennese style. The young people in Ihne's office had been quietly allowed to do what they wanted to do and Neoclassicism was the style to which Berlin architecture was then tending. A block further to the south, in Behrenstrasse, revealed and in part still does reveal the genesis of Berlin Neoclassicism: the big banks, which put up their palatial buildings here between the 1880s and the beginning of the First World War, adopted Neoclassicism earlier than the state, as can be seen, for instance, from the extensions to the Discontogesellschaft at the corners of Unter den Linden, Charlottenstrasse, and Charlottenstrasse/Behrenstrasse. Two banks in Behrenstrasse were by Messel, the Berliner Handelsgesellschaft and the Nationalbank. His biographers Karl Scheffler and Walter Behrendt ascribe to him the major share in the emergence of Berlin Neoclassicism, but they already point out that Peter Behrens superceded him in this. Criticism with this degree of penetration and skill was an essential part of the general situation in architecture in Berlin at that time.

Peter Behrens then gave expression to Berlin (and German) Neoclassicism in such a way that it became an internationally acknowledged, perhaps leading movement in art. What Messel did for the distribution monopoly, Behrens did for the production monopoly. The major step was of course his appointment as artistic advisor to AEG, a major electrical and mechanical engineering concern, in the autumn of 1907 (roughly at the same time as the foundation of the 'Deutsche Werkbund'). Behrens was given the task of designing or supervising the entire production plant. After the textile industry and the coal, iron and steel industry, mechanical engineering was bringing a third wave of industrialisation and AEG was playing a leading part in this, comparable perhaps to the part played by Ford in the USA. This wave of industrialisation culminated in the ultimate supremacy of the concerns, monopolies and big banks and it also put Germany beside England and the USA in the forefront of world trade. These preliminary remarks are necessary, for Behrens' work for AEG would have acquired historical significance of the first rank if only for this reason, quite apart from its artistic achievement.

Behrens' first famous turbine factory in Moabit, 1909, is rightly featured in many histories of modern architecture as one of the crucial factors in the development of twentieth-century architecture. Generally and regrettably, however, it is

3 Entrance to the Wertheim Department Store. One of six main arches, 1904 (second phase): 'part of the entrance to the city centre.'

4 Detail of the first phase of the Wertheim Department Store, 1904: 'such sublimation.'

5 Part of the first phase facade on Leipziger Strasse to the Wertheim Department Store, 1896: 'little more than pillars and glass.'

6 In the foreground the Disconto Gesellschaft, 1902, by W. Martins, and in the background a side view of the Staatsbibliothek, Unter den Linden, 1905-10, by Ernst v. Ihne: 'tasteful Neo-Baroque.'

7 AEG Turbine Hall, Huttenstrasse, Moabit, 1909, by Peter Behrens: 'first and foremost Neoclassical.'

8 Interior of the later AEG factory in Hussitenstrasse, Wedding, 1910-12, by Behrens.

seen only in connection with New Objectivity ('Neue Sachlichkeit') and Functionalism. The turbine factory is not objective at all; it is first and foremost Neoclassical, and is extremely expressive. Seen from the outside, its visible flank consists of colossal sheet-iron supports on which a huge, altogether trough-shaped roof rests on an iron cornice appearing at the front like a huge concrete roof or a stone on a giant's grave. The dramatic expression is intensified by the powerful corner stones which are obliquely supported on the interior, and the glass areas of the flanks leaning inwards reveal the way the steel supports then widen upwards. All this is as effective as it is unobjective: the building is an assembly hall for a heavy bridge crane, the main part of which is the track, invisible about three-quarters of the way up the window except in the evening when work is in progress by electric light and it appears as a dark strip. An objective architecture should have let the crane track be seen as Behrens did two years later in his next assembly shed, the AEG works in Brunnenstrasse in Wedding; the glass caterpillar of the skylight, visible from some distance, clearly shows that the roof stone is only a means of expression, not a truly solid object. Expression and illusion are two very different things, and Behrens had no intention of creating an illusion with his architecture.

The interpretation of the turbine factory as part of the New Objectivity movement was nourished by the material used: the huge glass areas, the concrete in the gable and the base, and above all the iron. It was Behrens' aim to give these new materials aesthetic expression. From that point of view, the bent and rather rough concrete panels of the corners which have something like a dressed-stone surface are the least successful parts, but the huge knee-high cast-iron foot joints of the girders are particularly fine. In the handling of these means of expression Behrens would appear to have gone further than any other European architect and to stand alongside the great Americans.

Especially in industrial building is the change of architectural style in Berlin very striking. The Schinkel school had adapted the English brick pillar and cap factories to its own use and the style had spread to such an extent that the roof construction had acquired the name 'Prussian cap' in central Europe. The dark red brick factories with their flat arched windows and cast-iron frames, buttresses and short cornices were interpreted as an architectural reduction (the contemporary term was 'Bedürfnisbau' – emergency building); I would suggest calling them 'Alte Sachlichkeit', (Old Objectivity). Unfortunately the

cast-iron internal supports hardly ever played a part in the external architecture. But the fine railway platforms with their cast-iron pillars, wire ties and wooden trusses covered with boards and tar paper are a compensation. This purpose-architecture of bricks, cast-iron and wood was regarded even by Messel's generation as obsolete. The city of Berlin appointed Ludwig Hoffmann as civic architect in order to get away from this style in its schools, hospitals and markets, and lift public building artistically above the mere response to need. Hoffmann's answer was a transmutation of high architecture into a well-groomed historicism. Behrens now – as far as I can see for the first time in monumental dimensions – replaced the brick walls and arched windows in industrial building with sheets of glass between iron supports.

The material and the individual forms in the turbine factory say a great deal about the ideas Behrens wished to convey. Here the supports are probably the most expressive: the I-profiles. In older industrial building in the cast-iron period, the supports, reduced in form, did, however, still remain antique columns. 'Old Objectivity' was a reduction but it was still historical, still classical architecture. The cast-iron and the bricks are only the means with which a form is created and the form still derives from concepts which have an historical legitimacy. In these 'Old Objective' and sparsely-decorated factories, the overladen cupboards, velvet door curtains, porcelain and door handles produced then now fill junk shops.

The I-profiles of the turbine factory have nothing in common with antique columns; they follow the logic of the rolling-mill. These are not old forms put to modern use and thus legitimising it; they are new forms which claim the dignity of the old in Behrens' classical arrangement. That would appear to be characteristic of the products which Behrens designed as well, the finest example being the famous arc lamps: claiming neither to be of particularly expensive material nor of antique profile, these are nevertheless first-class examples of applied art. So the design of these products and of the turbine factory was not intended to meet the naturally traditional taste of buyers. It claimed for the mass products of heavy industry and the mass production process that rank which hitherto had only been accorded to the higher bourgeois ideal, free art.

As early as 1913, Behrens' biographer, Fritz Hoeber, declared categorically that AEG with its world-wide interests was not dependent on advertising; rather, its products would match technical precision with aesthetic form. This is almost a

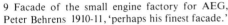

9 Facade of the small engine factory for AEG, Peter Behrens 1910-11, 'perhaps his finest facade.'

10 Project for the Embassy of the German Reich in St. Petersburg (Leningrad), 1911-12: 'the cultural leadership of the AEG monopoly became official.'

theological argument. Hoeber gives us the early functionalist ideology: 'beauty created out of purpose', 'the beauty of precision' and in the same breath he compares these factories with cathedrals. On the one hand it may have been a sign of progress that in this 'New Objective' art, society was becoming aware of industrialisation. On the other hand, the historical forms which had been abandoned may have pointed to a 'humanitas' which could have served economic and technical progress. Historical grandeur was felt to be phony, but did the new element which found expression in the I-profiles, for all its much-praised honesty, have reference only to itself? And could it then not be forced upon us as a standard? If it did not point beyond itself to those who had conceived it, those who had produced it and those for whom it was made, then it would certainly dominate and terrorise us, as it has indeed now done.

To be more precise, we can distinguish between several different strands in the social-industrial consciousness of Behrens' design. To consumers it had to be made clear that mass-produced objects were as elegant and acceptable as those of the best old craftsmen. This aspect is that represented by 'New Objectivity' and it will remain of world-wide significance as long as the big concerns operate. A further aspect is of a more national character. The industrial self-awareness evident in the gigantic drama of the turbine factory was the result of industrial achievement (huge turbines were to be assembled here), but whose self-awareness was it and in relation to whom? Firstly, certainly, the building reflects the pride of the owners of AEG and their management, the upper bourgeoisie who had just taken the German economy to the top of the world table with their modern organisational methods. Their demonstration was directed at the time firstly to the still-monarchical Prussian-German 'Junker' state. The time was ripe for the new class of industrial leaders, monopolists and big financiers to take an appropriate part in state affairs, and that meant playing a leading and decisive part. Behrens' work is not only a monument to this claim, but soon was able to reflect its successful fulfilment in what was perhaps his finest facade, the front of the small engine factory for the AEG works in Brunnenstrasse (1910-11). This was used the following year as the model for the Embassy of the German Reich which Behrens built in St. Petersburg. In other words, it can be said that the cultural leadership of the AEG monopoly became official.

It is only in describing these major achievements in architecture that it has become clear to what extent the system of the facades of Messel's Wertheim building and Behrens' turbine factory and small engine factory are similar: colossal skeleton columns, the ceilings of the storeys (or the crane track) set back, and the roof broken in the mansard style forming a plastic unity with the cornice. In these proudly rearing, and at the same time massive forms, the two architects found expression for a great moment in the development of the German upper bourgeoisie. One can hardly condemn the captains of industry for their desire for power and I am convinced that if they had acted otherwise, we would not have had such an impressive architectural testimony to their position. But I will go into this point in more detail later.

First I should like to spend a little more time on my interpretation of Behrens' Neoclassical version of this form. Colossal classical pillars are an imperial motif and reflect not only imperial claims in Germany but in the world as well. Le Corbusier has already commented on this with regard to the turbine factory, and one cannot blame a leading industrial nation for wishing to exert political influence and standing wherever its exports or imports were concerned. If one is to illustrate the catastrophe which Germany brought on her neighbours and herself and the role of the bourgeoisie as it was reflected in architecture – and that is our intention here – then the now-familiar reference to the relation between Berlin Neoclassicism, especially Behrens' work, and the classicism of the National Socialists is not entirely wrong, but it is too simple.

In the few years between the foundation of the 'Werkbund' and the outbreak of the First World War there was a *peripeteia*, a rise and fall, of the German bourgeoisie which can be traced with astonishing exactness in architecture. It can be seen in Behrens' industrial buildings and even more clearly in his administration buildings. However, we would like to trace it in residential building and so consider a further essential part of architecture in Berlin at the turn of the century.

In bourgeois residential building in Berlin at the turn of the century, the country house became the determinant model. To estimate the significance of this, we must take a brief look at residential building during the nineteenth century whose most characteristic form, certainly in terms of quantity, was the famous Berlin rented apartment block. Its architecture by no means had the clarity or uniformity of its designation and economic function; on the contrary, the apartment block was by heritage a bourgeois house, a development under patriarchal Prussian Absolutism from the medieval bourgeois house. It had acquired during the course of this development a

11 Apartment building facades: 'presented themselves to their sovereign's eye like a regiment of soldiers on parade.'

number of apartments for lodgers ('Einliegerwohnungen'), enforced by the absolutist administration in the eighteenth century as part of its encouragement of manufacturing. The bourgeois house generally had a shop on the ground floor to the street. Above the shop lived the petty patriarch, the owner of the house, in the *belle étage*, the windows of the 'best room' looking out on to the street and the dining room (the 'Berliner Zimmer') looking on to the courtyard, as did the rooms in which the family really lived, the bedrooms, nursery, kitchen, sewing room and so on. The servants' quarters were naturally at the back. The 'lodgers' had apartments in the second storeys which had become the rule towards the end of the eighteenth century, the better apartments facing the street and apartments for the lower income-groups looking out on to the courtyard. Until very recent times these families have been regarded as inferior and subject to the supervision of the landlord. At the back of the court there were workshops, and during the second 'Keiserreich' there were factories, each occupying one storey and rented out to different firms. The tenement houses of this period simply had a deeper plot, often with several side wings and hence several backyards. Some of them had no workshops. These houses, like the apartment blocks for the better classes, were now all five storeys.

These patriarchal houses with their architecturally-sophisticated facades and well-kept rooms looking out on to the street presented themselves to their sovereign's eye like a regiment of soldiers on parade. The historians' recognition that Absolutism was a necessary preliminary to the bourgeois age (in other words, liberal capitalism) is reflected in architecture in that this type of building remained the norm throughout the nineteenth century. Its facades and 'best rooms' – now called the 'salon' – were no longer perfectly suited to face the eyes of the absolutist ruling class but had to face the no less critical eyes of the bourgeois public and express reputation as 'credit'. (My landlord, complaining at the fact that we had no curtains, said :'In the flat upstairs you can see the money hanging at the window!') This type of house appears to have developed wherever the late Absolutist period reigned: there are, for example, similar houses in Paris.

Despite court precedence, the bourgeoisie had nothing of the equality of the sexes, so there were neither dual suites nor a central entrance. Where an apartment house did have such a central entrance, it would have been a double house. That this type of dwelling was well-suited to the bourgeoisie can be best illustrated by the fact that the bourgeois villa in Berlin, which emerged about 1800, gradually emancipated itself from the model of the pleasure-lodge or country seat of the nobility by adopting the form of the town house in a number of consistent stages of development: the 'salon' in front (where a garden now lent more dignity to the facade), the dining-room in the rear, the entrance at the side, bedrooms that had previously been *en suite* with the best rooms removed to the upper floor with the nursery and the utility rooms (coach-house and stables) at the back in the courtyard (which simply took its name from the town-house but was not really a courtyard at all). This type of villa had fully developed by about 1860, when the liberal bourgeoisie entered into its last trial of strength with the Prussian 'Junker' state over the constitution. After the defeat of the bourgeoisie and the victory of Bismarck it stagnated until about 1890.

But about 1890 it began to develop rapidly. The new houses had a two-storey entrance hall, or for the less well-to-do, a one-storey entrance hall was composed in concert with the staircase, which in addition to its function as the central crossing-point in the house was also more or less lived in. This meant that the Berlin bourgeois villa – now generally called a 'Landhaus' (country house) – was at last, and late indeed, completely emancipated from the court and absolutist model.

We need not ask whether the feudal heritage of its predecessor, the English country house, was forgotten or whether it had been deliberately abandoned in a sense of class independence. Even more important is the change in the bourgeois pattern of living itself, which is clearly reflected in the introduction of the hall. Especially in the most opulent houses with big two-storey halls, the upper gallery contained the bedrooms. In the liberalist villa – what I would like to call the type which emerged and declined between 1860 and 1890 organised on the lines of the town-house – a rigorous separation was maintained between the rooms in which guests were received and the rest of the house. The children who were not yet 'out' or ready for society, for instance, were never allowed to enter these rooms without being accompanied by an adult. The women did no house work at all here (with the possible exception of embroidery). Thus, the division between private and public life went right through the house. The patriarchal liberal of the old school lived, one might say, a dual existence: to the outside world and as far as the salon he was a liberal, an equal meeting equals, but in the family the strictest hierarchy was maintained. At the turn of the century the 'Landhaus' with its hall reflected a desire for a freer and more unified, less contradictory way of life.

What had formerly been external pressure became an inherent civilisation, civility. The border between public and private life was no longer between the 'best rooms' and those used every day but was at the threshold of every room used by every member of the family. In the English house this had meant that every room had only one door, there were no longer suites of reception rooms. The German country house never reached this culmination, civility never became quite so perfect here. *Nevertheless, there has never again been in Germany such a cultured way of life.*

The finest example of this type of house which we were still able to see (before it was recently converted to small owner-occupier flats) was Muthesius' Haus Neuhaus in Dahlem, built in 1906. Entering the hall from the entrance to the house, the visitor had a ceiling above him; on his left the hall disappeared into a half-lit area (leading to the kitchens, serving-rooms and so on). To the right was the brightly lit, two-storey part of the hall, where an open fire with benches on both sides formed a resting place and focal point, partly concealed by a projecting part of the landing. Posener has called the hall Muthesius' most important room. The deep alcove in which the door from the gentlemen's room to the ladies' room was set fulfilled the function of creating distance. And the sub-division of the

13 Ground plan of the Wilhelm von Bode house, 1885, by H. Grisebach: An example of a liberal villa.

12 Street facade of the Wilhelm von Bode house, 1885.

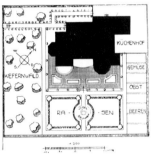

14 Site layout of Haus Neuhaus, 1906-07, by H. Muthesius: 'there has never again been such a cultured way of life in Germany.'

15 Street facade of Haus Neuhaus, Dahlem, Berlin.

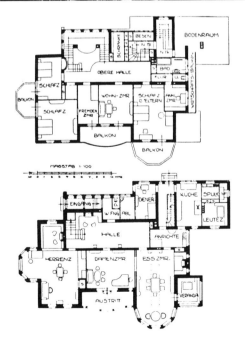

16 Entrance hall to Haus Neuhaus: 'Muthesius' most important room'

17 Ground and first floor plan of Muthesius' Haus Neuhaus, Dahlem, 1906-07.

45

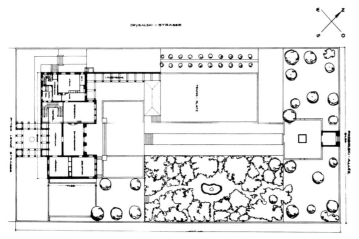

18 Plan of Haus Theodor Wiegand, archaeologist, Dahlem, 1911-12, by P. Behrens: 'this house clearly turns its back on any kind of public.'

19 Street facade of Haus Theodor Weigand: 'a solemn peristyle stands before the entrance.'

gentlemen's room into areas for concentrated work, areas for relaxation, confidential discussion – these people knew how to handle their luxury. There was perhaps less individuality in the arrangement of the ladies' room. Apparently the house was inhabited by several pairs of members of the same family – perhaps grandparents, or perhaps married children.

In these houses the servants' quarters, too, were designed with care and consideration: the staff worked in a separate kitchen wing on the ground floor and slept on the top floor. In the liberalist villa they had generally worked and slept in unhealthy basements in wretched conditions. This took its revenge on the building in that the basement (needing light) had to reach so high above stairs that the natural relation between the house and the garden was rarely achieved. Both the house and the garden were spoilt, and the integration of life in the house with life in the garden, which is the point of the villa, was hardly possible. It was not until the beginning of the twentieth century that the best examples of the country house were at last built flat on the ground.

About 1905, the country house was reaching its culmination in works like these by Muthesius, and became the determinant model for the city. The best rented apartment blocks in the west end of Berlin now had a wood-panelled entrance hall (instead of the pilastered entrances to be found in the best of the earlier houses, for instance, those of the factory owners in Kreuzberg), a lift, and in each of the apartments an entrance that widened to a hall before the salon.

The liberalist villa, as we said, was organised along the lines of the town-house. The suburbs with their villas in those days were improved versions of cities, expressing no hostility to urban life or civilisation. The country house, however, leaves room for hostility to urban life and culture, which can amount to an anti-bourgeois attitude. Even the name, country house, suggests a flight from the city. In this connection the aesthetic relation between the house and its plot of land is interesting. Muthesius' houses 'An der Rehwiese' or his 'Haus Cramer' are beside public parks; they utilise the view over the park, reaching out into the park optically and spatially. Conversely, 'Haus Neuhaus' stands on a relatively small plot of land. Muthesius incorporated the garden with a terrace and balustrade into his architecture. Today, where the garden has fallen victim to the conversion of the house, one can suddenly see that the house is too big for the plot of land it stands on. It now seems as ugly and clumsy as most of the houses in villa suburbs up to today. What makes the house ugly is its unrealistic pretension to stand in a lonely and empty space.

This explains why the more civilised West European terraced house made so little impression on Berlin.

With the country house the relation to the outside world also becomes more distant. Muthesius' own house stands between the Potsdamer Chaussee and the Rehwiese but is turned towards the quiet landscape. 'Haus Neuhaus' has a strip of pine wood between its garden and the street and the garden is beside the house, not in front of it. Certainly the Potsdamer Chaussee was no longer the public thoroughfare it had once been, when the Chancellor Prince Hardenberg or Prince Karl of Prussia, who also had summer residences on this street, had their garden houses and belvederes here. With the coming of the railways, some of the traffic had long moved to another track; and at the turn of the century, those who travelled down the Chaussee were in fast-moving motor cars and could no longer be recognised and greeted.

This is not to dispute the peak of German bourgeois culture and German civilisation which had been reached at this point, but is only to point out that the external conditions and forms of the country house at least permitted less civilised alternatives. The political and economic data can quickly be outlined. It is generally recognised that the basis of liberalism was the independence of the many self-employed. Later, the monopolies, industrial concerns and big banks dominated the economy and the basis of bourgeois freedom was jeopardised. The same problem appeared internationally in all the industrial countries, but what followed was specific to Germany.

After Bismarck had broken the back of German liberalism, the movement proved incapable of regeneration, for its economic basis had gone. The culture of the villa with its hall can certainly be interpreted as a second generation phenomenon which had risen in and profited from the age of industrialisation at the end of the nineteenth century. This class was on the threshold of political power and it was ready to make itself felt on the world stage. Should it rely patiently on the support of a weak bourgeoisie, an urban civility and freedom, or should it not simply form an alliance with the feudal military of the Prussian 'Junkertum' (the landowners in the country): this alternative would seem to be indicated in the contradictory features of the country house. *Societies and social classes are often forced by historical circumstances to make decisions regardless of how well they can prepare themselves.*

Everyone knows how the choice was made. It decided the fate of the nation and it was made without external pressure for internal reasons. It is reflected in yet another change in the style of living of the upper bourgeoisie and in the design of their

20 Project for the garden facade of Haus Theodor Wiegand: 'the gardens seem even more serious, heavy and formal than the entrance.'

houses. Around 1910 the relaxed, indecisive and pluralistic design of the country house with its hall comes to an end. It is followed by the most decisive turn-around in the history of the German bourgeois villa. From now on the villa turns its back on the street, acts as a barrier to the garden. It again uses a central entrance. The living rooms are now facing on to the garden at the rear, the utilities (the garage and the rubbish bins) are at the front. All this has lasted to the present day. Historically it is all analogous to the late-absolutist *maison de plaisance* of the eighteenth century. The country house again has suites of reception rooms; Posener calls this development reactionary and states regretfully that even Muthesius was not able to remain untouched by it. However, the main protagonist was Behrens; this can very clearly be seen from the house he built for the 'Oberbürgermeister' (mayor) of Hagen, Cuno, in Eppenhausen in 1909, which, despite its corner situation, has no living room windows on the streets and is designed like a fortress. The house has a front entrance, is altogether symmetrical, the large hall is gone and the living rooms are *en suite*.

More highly differentiated is Behrens' famous house for the archeologist and son-in-law of Siemens, Wiegand, in Dahlem, 1911, built in the style of a Greek temple, the house consists of solid limestone blocks with a solemn peristyle entrance. Nothing was to be light in this house. Clumsy architectural features such as the indecisive and unhappy position of the stairs, the lack of space in the organisation of the utility rooms, the fact that the serving door is visible from the entrance to the dining room, should not be over-emphasised (Behrens was an accomplished painter and graphic artist); nevertheless, this lack of consideration for everyday concerns seems coarse immediately after Muthesius' extreme delicacy and sensitivity.

What does reflect the full and deliberate intentions of the builder and architect, however, is the squat, rather square shape of the rooms. Together with the serious and heavy panelling, the doors and their handles, this gives the whole a formality and stiffness which does not permit a relaxed way of life. The living quarters of the house (not counting the utility wing and the pergolas) have a solemn symmetry to the garden and the centre part of the front has colossal pilasters; but the garden front is not visible from outside. The house stands on a corner site, but Behrens has included a utility yard to the side street and also a pergola which deviates from the perspective in that it is actually walled to its full height. Although there would seem to be little reason for this, the garden seems even more serious, heavy and formal than the entrance and the salons,

owing to the colossal order and the symmetry of the front of the house. This upper bourgeois house clearly turns its back on any kind of public, but behind its heavy doors decisions were taken which affected society. Weigand is said to have built the house to be able to invite the Kaiser. He was the great archaeological organiser who, following in the footsteps of German imperialism in the south-east (the Baghdad railway) 'cleaned up the Near East for Germany', as an archaeologist once said in conversation. It is remarkable how well his main acquisitions, monuments of Hellenist imperialism – the Pergamon altar, the market gate of Milet – fitted into the German scene. It is the same Wiegand who fought to have building on the Messel's Pergamon museum continue in the 1920s; it is still not finished today, but remains the main monument to the imperialism of the German 'Kaiserreich'.

Of course there is no lack of average examples. Anyone who goes in search of these should look at the entrance hall to the marine office of 1911, in which the short-sighted naval policy makers of the late 'Kaiserreich' had offices. Residential building for workers, white-collar workers and civil servants, public transport, city parks, even town-planning itself were all subject to major new impulses during these years which have remained of primary importance right up to the present, and they deserve more detailed discussion.[1] We have dealt with some of those significant aspects giving some indication of the situation to which the 'Werkbund' and its members should have submitted; but of course they did not. This we know all too well now.

Translated from the German by Eileen Martin.

Editor's note:
1. Such a more detailed discussion can be understood by referring to the recently published book by Prof. J. Posener, *Berlin – Auf Dem Wege Zu Einer Neuen Architektur – Das Zeitalter Wilhelms II*, Prestel Verlag, Munich.

Goerd Peschken
Born in 1931 at Nordhausen in Thuringia and studied at a humanistic 'Gymnasium'; was a carpenter's and cabinet-maker's apprentice for two years and then studied architecture, his most impressive teachers having been Egon Eiermann, Hans Scharoun and Otto Ernst Schweizer and the historians of architecture Ernst Heinrich, Heinrich Lenzen and Arnold Tschira. Undertook archaeological work in Greece and the Orient, and wrote criticism on the devastation of historical cities by town-planning for periodicals. Still writes as an expert on authorities of state, together with Tilmann Heinisch. Has also done studies on Karl Friedrich Schinkel, a doctoral thesis and a major book entitled Architektonisches Lehrbuch. *Other areas of interest include the former Berlin Stadtschloss by Andreas Schlüter and others, historical town-planning and building typology (mainly using the examples of Berlin). Currently Professor für Baugeschichte in Hamburg, Hochschule für bildende Kunste.*

Tilmann J. Heinisch
Born in 1941 in Gloppingen/Württemberg and studied architecture under the auspices of Egon Eiermann, Arnold Tschira and Franzsepp Wurtenberger. Taught as Wissenschaftlicher Assistant in Karlsruhe and at the Technische Universität Berlin, and is undertaking studies on the genesis of domestic architecture and on historical town-planning. Works in collaboration with Goerd Peschken as an architect and as a writer of architectural theory.

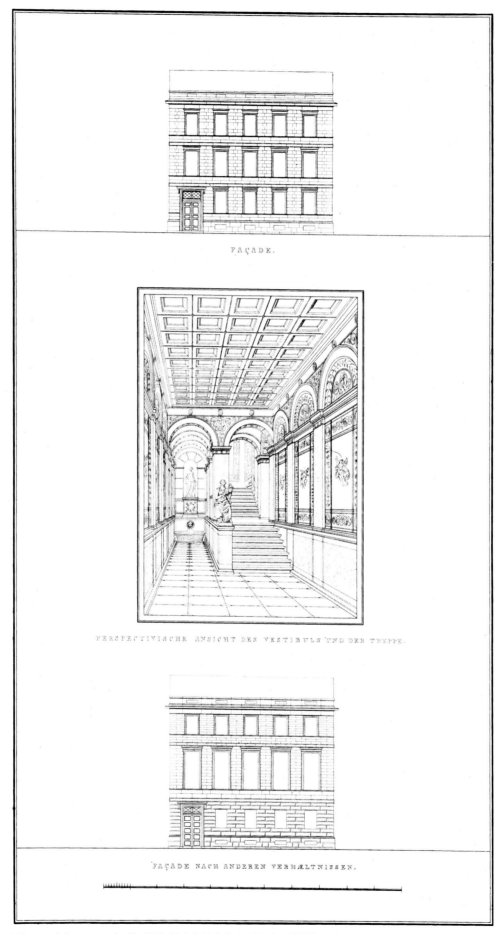

FAÇADE.

PERSPECTIVISCHE ANSICHT DES VESTIBULS UND DER TREPPE.

FAÇADE NACH ANDEREN VERHÆLTNISSEN.

1 Bourgeois house type by Karl Friedrich Schinkel, the King's official architect in 1825.

Goerd Peschken
The Berlin 'Miethaus' and Renovation

I have spoken several times before professional circles and once to the general public on the subject of the Berlin 'Mietshaus' (apartment house) and renovation.[1] The subject is still a crucial one. Fortunately, general protest has stopped the total demolition of all the quarters of West Berlin with nineteenth-century apartment houses but whole areas of the city are still nevertheless being destroyed; and those buildings which are left standing are being completely converted. Behind the old facades they are adjusted to the present standards of social housing with the same interiors and fittings as new housing while being let at the same rents.

This transformation of the old quarters of Berlin is in my view the greatest social and cultural retrogression since the Federal Republic of Germany came into being. The view held in architectural circles and by the general public that the 'Berliner Mietskaserne' (rented barracks) was a slum and the main cause of the dreadful housing conditions in the nineteenth century is certainly not the reason for the transformation; however, it helps to justify it. In my lectures and in this article I am aiming to question this view.

The Evolution of the Apartment House

Architecturally, the Berlin apartment houses of the last century were certainly not cheap housing for the poor, they were a stage of development of the 'Bürgerhaus' (bourgeois house) from which they represented a smooth transition. Like all North German cities, the domestic architecture of Berlin in the Middle Ages consisted of gabled houses. Historically these houses were a variant of the northwest German 'Hallenhaus', which as its name suggests, mainly consisted of one large room, the hall or threshing-floor. When I was a student in Berlin in the 1950s one of these houses was still standing in the medieval part of the city at Fischerstrasse 32. It has now been demolished.[2] Fischerstrasse was in a lower middle-class district. The owner of the house may have been a boat-builder or net-maker or perhaps even a fisherman. Presumably the house had always had an upper storey. In the hall the dividing walls were clearly secondary, the roof beams spanning directly from one outside wall to the other while the staircase was not in a clearly-defined place. The buttress construction of the outside walls marked the house as being of the Middle Ages. In this single room, a patriarchal family once produced goods. The journeymen and maid-servants lived in the house like the children of the family, eating and sleeping there, and living under the supervision of the parents.

Production in the house later declined or ceased altogether and the house became apartments for several families. The rear wing had been built to rent out. Built in a straight section, it had eight apartments with parlours, while a smaller room and cooking facilities could be found in the hall. The apartments were built in pairs and two families always had cooking facilities next to each other in the hall; the front of the house had a small apartment on the ground floor and a larger one upstairs, and there was a ninth apartment in a little side

building. The rear wing before demolition had a mansard roof, a form which only became the general pattern in Berlin in the eighteenth century, so it would appear that it was during the eighteenth century that the house was converted. By that date, the owner had ceased to operate as a medieval craftsman directing a small family business.

By the eighteenth century the Berlin 'Bürgerhaus' was already a house with gutters rather than a house with front gate. The absolutist ruler enforced roof guttering for greater protection against the spread of fire and as an aid to the street police. Guttered houses were separated by a party wall between the house-tops, and the previously common gutter at street level, in which it was easy to hide from the police and make an escape, was no longer deemed necessary. The city council resisted such changes, and although they would no doubt have preferred greater protection against fire, the council itself was made up of 'Bürgers' and therefore no further pressure was possible by the king: too much prestige attached to the front gable. The well-known plan by Johann Bernhard Schultz of 1685 shows how many guttered houses had already been built in Berlin by then.[3] Around 1700 Martin Grünberg, the Royal engineer, worked to accelerate the introduction of guttered houses; he designed two 'Bürgerliche Wohnhäuser' (bourgeois houses) and the designs were engraved and published.[4] One of the houses has as a compromise a gabled dormer window. The use of the term 'Wohnhäuser' (houses) shows that production had been moved out of the house itself into sheds in the yard. On the ground floor of the front house, however, there would still have been a shop and offices. The designation of the entrance to the yard as 'Tenne' (the old hall or threshing-floor)

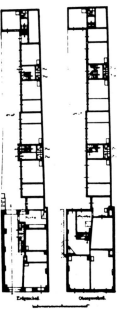

2 The last house from the Middle Ages in Fischerstrasse, now demolished.

3 Bourgeois house type by the King's master builder Grünberg, about 1700.

4, 5 House for the owner of a factory: the Nicolas House, Brüderstrasse.

and the indefinite placing of the stairs point back to the origin of this type of house. Other new elements, apart from the gutter, are the stucco on the facade, and the arrangement of the reception rooms in the upper storey on the street front; these features were all adopted from court culture. The stucco facade and the suite of rooms show the owner to be a small patriarch modelling himself on the great patriarch, the Prince, who had a great Baroque stucco facade (although this also contained a lot of quarry stone) and huge suites of rooms in his palace.

The people who rented apartments in Fischerstrasse 32 worked outside the house, and the well-to-do citizens had thus changed the cottage industry of the smaller craftsmen into factory production. The house in Brüderstrasse 13, for example, belonged to the owner of a manufactory (it is still standing, thanks to the preservation authorities in the GDR).[5] Brüderstrasse was in a wealthy quarter of the medieval city. About the middle of the eighteenth century the house belonged to the manufacturer Gotzkowsky, who among other things founded the Berlin porcelain works. In 1788 it was bought by the book-dealer and publisher Nicolai, and it was probably then that the house acquired its present form. On the ground floor and in the buildings in the yard, people who rented apartments in Fischerstrasse would have worked. The magnificent carved oak staircase led to the richly furnished

rooms on the upper storey looking on to the street. It was in these rooms that the owner of the house received his guests. Unfortunately, the ground-plan does not show the rear wings with the workshops and the rooms for the servants, for in addition to those who came in from outside to work, there were some who slept in the house. The entrance to the yard, the position of the stairs to the yard, and the arrangement of the best rooms at the front of the house were then characteristic of this type of house and remained so until the beginning of the twentieth century.

Very few citizens of Berlin were as wealthy as Nicolai. The self-employed of the next lower rank were still subject to the Royal building policy until around 1800. The king may well have provided wood, stones and the site for the building, but he certainly prescribed what the facade had to look like and the detailed design of the front house. Many collections contain designs for what were known as 'Immediatbauten'[6] – building on immediate, ie direct order of the king, who in this case went straight to the citizens and circumvented the municipal authorities. In the 'Residenzstadt' there were many people who were not engaged in trade or commerce. According to the civic constitution, some were not empowered to build a house for themselves, while others could not afford to do so. They were lesser officials at court (corresponding to civil servants today),

6 Facade of a house built under direct orders of the king, 1776.

members of the nobility who only wanted to spend a few years in Berlin, envoys from foreign princes or representatives of trading companies, and so on. Finally there were the day labourers and soldiers of every rank.

The state was concerned to see that there was an adequate supply of rented accommodation to house these people. Some of the designs for 'Immediatbauten' are for four-storey houses. Assuming that the owner will have lived on the first floor, this means that there must have been at least two more (probably less expensive) apartments to let on the upper floors. On the ground floor there may have been perhaps two shops; again the owner will only have used one, so the other was to rent. In the attics of the rear wing, which the owner could build to his own requirements, lived soldiers; outside the hours needed for military exercise, they were under the supervision of the owner of the house and did manual work, carried messages etc. Officers naturally lived in the front of the house. It is this enforced billeting that is said to have given rise to the term 'Mietskaserne' (rented barracks).

About 1825 Schinkel designed 'Bürgerhäuser', and like those of Grünberg, his designs were published by the state.[7] But Schinkel's designs were recommendations, not direct orders from the king. Schinkel's design is only for a three-storey house and in a sense he may have been turning the clock back a

little. In the accompanying text he regrets that there are no single-family houses left in Berlin, town palaces as one might say, where (as he indicates at the foot of the drawing) the reception rooms were to be recognisable by their great windows. Unfortunately, the storeys had to be of more or less equal height because they contained rented apartments, all of which needed their reception rooms at the front. Schinkel's design has the usual suite of rooms at the front, which included the dining-room (although it looked out on to the courtyard: that was held to be feasible because the guests would be at the table). But Schinkel's design differs from what was and would remain the typical house design. In the Berlin apartment houses the 'Berliner Zimmer', in the corner to the rear wing, generally served as dining-room. Schinkel's dining-room by comparison is adjoined by a corridor which leads to the bedrooms, and right at the back beside the staircase to the servants' quarters is the kitchen to prevent any smells reaching the reception rooms. Schinkel also considerately puts the grown-up sons' rooms near those of the maids. The hall which does not lead through into the yard became the norm in wealthier districts towards the end of the century, but this did not apply to the interior staircase with a skylight, however. As the hall did not permit an entrance to the yard, this cannot have contained workshops, store-houses, coach-house or stables as in previous times. So the site

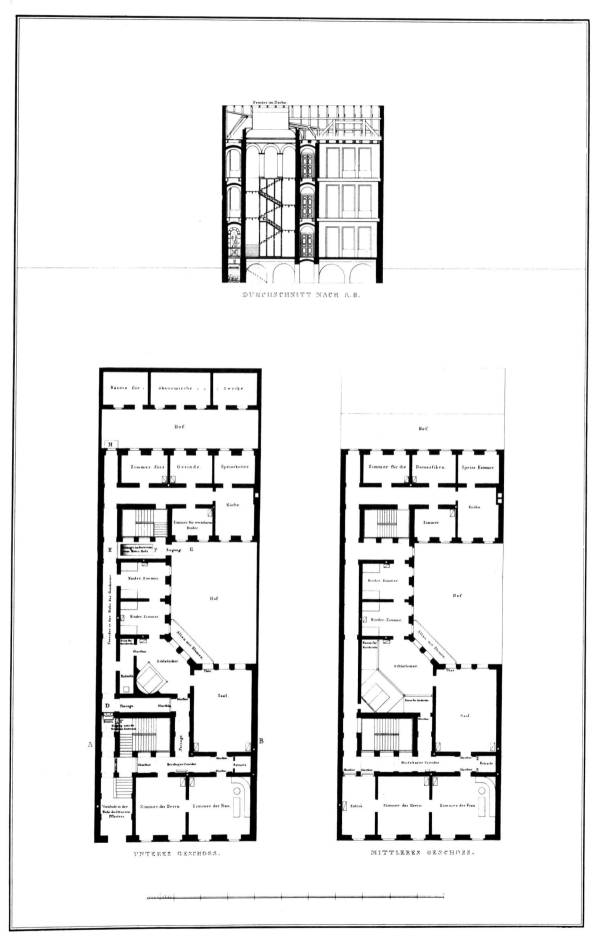

7 Bourgeois house type by Karl Friedrich Schinkel.

8 Houses for factory owners in Adalbertstrasse in 1860.

9 Courtyard of a house for a factory owner in Waldermarstrasse in 1860.

Schinkel had in mind would not have been used for production. In all likelihood the owner and main occupier would have been engaged in the services sector, as an official, a doctor, lawyer, agent or perhaps as a high-ranking officer in the army.

During the generation after Schinkel, Luisenstadt to the south-east was built as an extension to the centre of the city.[8] The houses follow Schinkel's classicism but they are five storey, not three storey, with a basement which was let as shops and apartments. Kreuzberg/Luisenstadt was a district inhabited by wealthy factory owners. Here production did go on in the space behind the houses. This can be seen from the entrances to the yards. However, the buildings in the yards are no longer the old two storey sheds, nor are any verandahs and little gardens left for us to see. These only survived in areas which did not develop a strong commercial activity, as in most areas of the district. After the 1880s it became the practice in Luisenstadt to build factory premises which could be rented storey by storey, so there were not only apartments to let in these houses but commercial premises as well. The traditional type of bourgeois house was changing more and more.

As a short digression: it is characteristic of the contemporary authorities' arbitrary method of working, that after the demolition of the Rollberge in Neukölln, a rather poor lower middle-class and working-class district, the next on the list for clearance was Luisenstadt, which was relatively old but in fact was a very good neighbourhood. This can be judged by its provision with parks and green areas and monumental buildings, some of them the best in Berlin. But Luisenstadt was not only an example of first-class quality in town planning. The houses were also of good architectural quality, the stucco was excellent and there were many fine doors and door handles. The entrances leading to the courtyards and the stairs were well formed and the property was in good order *before* the district was declared an official renovation area. This high state of repair was possible because the factory owners had always had access, even in difficult times, to labour and material to keep their houses in good repair.

Returning to the evolution of the apartment house, a generation later the characteristics had not greatly changed. Alt-Moabit 90, built in 1892, had first-class apartments.[9] The dual arrangement of the front houses had become usual in Kreuzberg and it had by this time become the norm. Beside the entrance at the front, but looking out onto the courtyard, was the living room used by the wife where she would do as she pleased. The two rooms looking onto the street were reception rooms. At most, the man of the house may have had a writing-desk here. The 'Berliner Zimmer' was the dining-room, followed by a corridor with bedrooms, kitchen and stairs to the servants' quarters. At the rear could be a few rooms for the family to use or which could form a separate apartment for a relative or a lodger.

It must be remembered that the reception rooms were scarcely ever used by the family and the children were virtually never allowed in. The wife could at most engage in some pastime such as embroidery: any other form of sewing or housework would have been unthinkable. The children only entered the rooms at Christmas or when they were introduced to visitors: washed, brushed and combed in their Sunday best. The everyday life of the family was spent in the rooms looking onto

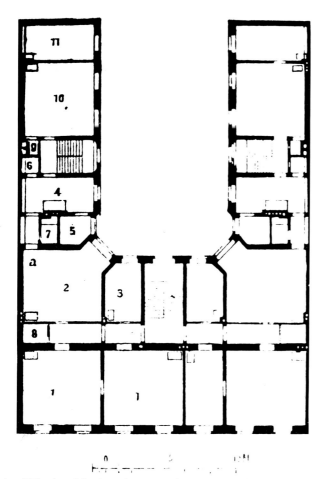

10 A middle-class *Mietshaus* (apartment house) type as illustrated in *Berlin und seine Bauten*, 1877.

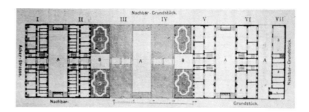

11, 12 The Meyer Apartment Building, Ackerstrasse, in 1874.

the courtyard, as was that of their servants. There was nothing negative about the architecture of the court and work went on there, carts loaded and unloaded, carpets were beaten and so on.

How did the workers live? Some were in the suburbs, in Neukölln, Schönberg, Charlottenburg, in smaller versions of the 'Bürgerhaus', but most of them were in districts directly adjoining the city, Prenzlauerberg, Friedrichshain, Wedding, Moabit, living in large houses with a great many small apartments in their backyards.[10] A particular type of working class house emerged around 1870. This was the cross-wing type, the most striking example of which is the Meyersche Hof, Ackerstrasse, 132/133 in Wedding.[11] These were six five-storey rows with small apartments, consisting of a parlour, a smaller room, and a kitchen; the smaller room and the kitchen were always on one side of a public central corridor and the parlour on the other. In the courtyards there were gardens alternating with toilets and refuse boxes. The side wing No. VII had commercial premises on two storeys and an apartment for the manager and bath-cabins which the tenants could use free of charge.

In the front of the house there were shops on the ground floor, and workshops on the ground floor of the last side section. In contemporary literature it was regretted that the splitting of the apartments through the common corridor destroyed the comfort of a self-contained dwelling. The sentiment was, as we shall see, rather hollow. The builder, a banker, was a practical man. He knew that his tenants could not pay the rent themselves and would have to take in lodgers. The parents slept in the kitchen. The lodgers slept in the parlour and the smaller room, and there therefore could be no question of a self-contained dwelling in any case. If possible, the small room was

let out during the day for one or two night-shift workers to sleep in.

In addition the wife and – after school – the children would have to do some kind of work at home: dress-making, sewing and so on. The size of most of the parlours is indicative of this. This complex was designed as an apartment house for workers and is a precursor of the modern row construction and of those housing estates with common utilities (I am thinking of the Socialist estates of the 1920s). The facade of Meyersche Hof was severe, but the house was technically well built and there was actually decorative carving round the windows of the stairs as in the best of the middle-class houses. So the substance had not been skimped. Unfortunately, most of the site was destroyed in the war and the wings which remained have now been demolished.

But this type did not become established as a working-class apartment house. Even in the working-class districts one finds almost exclusively houses of the bourgeois type. One example in Moabit, Emdener Strasse 27, 1889[12] will illustrate the system. The apartments in the front part of the house are for lower middle-class employees or skilled workers; they have a parlour, two smaller rooms and a kitchen and hence correspond to the 2½ room apartment now provided under the social housing programme. The pantry next to the kitchen does not go up the full height of the storey, so that the ventilation for the toilet can be taken across above it. One of the two front apartments can be extended up to the first back staircase. At the back, the toilets are outside the apartments on the landings.

Some of these back apartments consist of a parlour, smaller room and kitchen, while others have only a parlour and

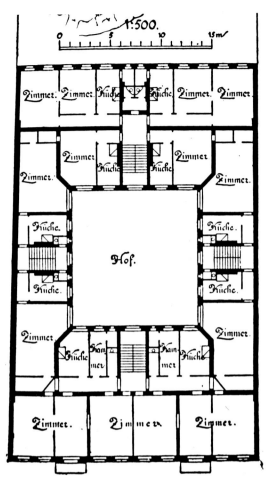

13 Workers' housing as illustrated in *Berlin und seine Bauten*, 1896.

kitchen. The toilet on the landing enables the apartment to be even further sub-divided and used as bed-sitters. The owner of the house preferred more prosperous tenants, not because he charged them more rent, but because the rent collection was less problematic and entailed less management. He would not lower the rent – poorer tenants had to share. From outside in the courtyard one can clearly see where the toilets are inside the apartments and where they are outside.

The facade of the house and the quality of the building in Emdener Strasse was virtually the same as that of the bourgeois apartment houses. In contemporary literature, especially in criticism of Berlin working-class housing about 1910, the quality of the stucco is held to be related to the mortgage speculation. Certainly the possibility of taking in better tenants added to the money value of the houses. But there were clear limits to the variability of the layout. A proper middle-class apartment could not have been created in a house like this.

There is a further related aspect which I would like to raise. These facades and the type of house had been the norm in the eighteenth century: then the facade had been the expression of the patriarchal claim of the owner in the great absolutist system, a claim to exercise authority over his servants, workers and so on, some of whom lived in this household (although, as we have seen, the custom was dying out). Certainly at that time the master felt a sense of responsibility towards the domestics and workers who lived under his roof. He would look after them if they were in need, although this help may not have been very generous. Although the circumstances had completely changed by the end of the nineteenth century, the stucco and architecture of these houses were still expressing the same

convention: the tenants were not engaged in any work or production process for the owner of the house, nor did he feel the remotest responsibility for their welfare. The only thing that had remained consistent was the oppression of these people who were turned out immediately if they did not pay the rent.

In what way were they oppressed? Very certainly part of their suffering consisted in the bad quality of the housing. Some of the backyards were very small and gave on to very dark apartments. The worst type of house was that in which the owner had no hope of finding better tenants: he did not build side wings because he saw no chance of being able to let front apartments which stretched into the side wing. Taking the ceilings and roof construction round the corner was structurally complicated and cost more. But if only cross-wings were built, the apartments at the back could have lower ceilings. Then the toilets were often outside on the landing for the front apartments as well, but this was only recognisable from the courtyard. From the front the stucco facade, symbol of bourgeois pretension, was the same as always.

The Facade as Signifier

So certainly there were very dark apartments in the back courtyards. But anyone who has any knowledge at all of the literature on housing in Berlin must know that the housing problem during the Kaiserreich was not mainly due to the bad quality of the houses. The courtyards show how little the lighting of the working-class apartments differed from that of the rooms in which the well-to-do families lived in their apartments. And it can also be shown, for instance, that the provision of toilets was only one generation behind that of the better houses. I know, for example, of Bürgerhäuser from the middle of the nineteenth century in a good neighbourhood, with a toilet on the stairs or in the courtyard.

The wretched housing conditions in Berlin were largely due to overcrowding, which is as good as saying they were due to excessive rents. This was proved and generally acknowledged by, at the latest, 1910.[13] At that time, academic critics had calculated that the houses, measured by normal commercial standards and wages (whatever that may have been), were as a rule 100% too expensive, so that the rents were on average twice as high as they should have been. This in turn caused twice as many people to be crowded into the apartments as they should have held. The present older generation can remember the problem of housing refugees from the eastern provinces and those who had been bombed out after the war. That was nothing in comparison with the housing problems of the Kaiserreich in Berlin. In those days people lived in cellars and tuberculosis was rife. Their strikes over rent were illegal and were suppressed by the state authorities. For a long time under Bismarck the workers were prevented from forming organisations to fight for higher wages. Bismarck was so consistent a patriarch that he caused the same State that enslaved the workers to introduce liability for cases of officially-defined need.

The conventional bourgeois facades therefore signified the conventional bourgeois claim to dominance, and they did so in the generally accepted architectural language of the time, the stucco facade. This bourgeois dominance was hated and it was indeed detestable. And so the facades of the apartment houses were deemed to be ugly. That, however, is a social and aesthetic judgement, not an architectural or formal one. The facades of the old apartment houses were detestable in the same way that the recently 'chic' investment apartment houses in Luisenstadt which block the view and devastate hope are detestable as well.

14 Facades of workers' housing, Putbuser Strasse, in 1880.

15 The worst type of workers' housing, The Courtyard, in 1880.

At the End of Speculation

During the Kaiserreich the inflation rate was so low that the critics of the mortgage speculation in apartment houses in Berlin argued that several generations of tenants would have to pay the exorbitant rents to provide the excessive profits demanded by the speculators. But things turned out differently. The Kaiserreich and its currency collapsed in the First World War. Domestic political conditions changed (at least over the short term) in favour of the workers. The interests of heavy industry, which had been the dominant factor in the economy for such a long time, had also registered that speculation was not in their interests, for the exorbitant rents resulted either in higher wages or less efficient workers, the latter condition caused by under-nourishment and sickness due to lack of money. Industry wanted neither of these. It needed healthy and cheap labour.

These arguments were already appearing in the housing literature of 1910, but it was only after the First World War was lost that they were accepted, when fear of revolution was very real. From then on subsidies were provided to ease the housing shortage – the modern equivalent is the social housing programme – and rent freezes were introduced. Although political history has been turbulent from the November Revolution in 1918 until the present day, the apartment houses of the Kaiserreich have long ceased to be an instrument and image of oppression. In 1960, the apartments certainly did not cost more than they were worth to those who lived in them, and that by association also made the houses less ugly.

*'The doll costs two marks and ten,
We thought it was good for that price.'*

Günter Grass

The owners now saw no point in the stucco and it was knocked off when the facades were being repaired. It was no longer a sign of a good bourgeois position or of authority over workers, at any rate not through an apartment and its rent. But where they have not been renewed, these facades now have a different message. Now that the oppressive – in 1910 it was

actually called dishonest – profit for the speculators has been taken, what remains is the honest work of many hands. And the traces of the suffering our people were subject to during the bombing raids, when the splinters flew and the foundations shook, and during the following years of hunger and cold, when the walls froze and the plaster fell off, have also made the houses more beautiful. I always thought they were beautiful, and I can now provide the social and aesthetic considerations to justify that view. The houses are an indication of a great hope in our society, the hope that it may be possible to take one aspect of life out of the commercial pressure to exploit everything. That is the finest thing about them.

The Berlin 'Mietshaus' was for forty years a problem that had largely been solved, and until sometime after 1960 it was a great social hope. The inhabitants paid what the apartments were worth and it could be taken that they would have paid a comparable price for improvements. Where the stucco facades had been preserved, they were a sight for sore eyes, a luxury we all could share, and the cracks in them were a testimony to our history, a part of us all. As students we used to imagine that the very narrow courtyards could be improved by knocking down one or the other wing – that was all that was needed.

The Oppression of Renovation

The hopes have proved vain. Domestic political conditions have enabled economic interests to take the houses over and they have been drawn into yet another process of commercial utilisation. Now it is no longer the old owners or their heirs, but new groups who are at work. The new process is called renovation. In every variant we have seen so far, renovation has brought a retrogression. Total clearance destroys all hope and even wipes out memory. I have heard Ernst May call the apartments in the fabulous new concrete tower blocks 'rabbit hutches'. Concrete blocks erected on sites where every trace of the old city has been wiped out are just about good enough for rabbits who have no memory and who hope for nothing.

What, we then must ask, remains in the case of individual renovation projects, when part of the building is preserved? Let us look at Hardt-Waltherr Hämer's hard-won renovation

16 'Renovation' of the Rollberge in Berlin Neukölln in 1971.

in Putbuser Strasse in Wedding. Most of the fronts of the houses are still standing, but here the regulations of the social housing programme apply. The same amount of green *must* be provided in the vicinity, the same number of parking spaces. At the rear and inside, everything *has* to be changed – the living rooms *have* to look out on to the parking space with its green surround.

While the work was going on there, I photographed a shed at the back of the site of one of the worst types of apartment house which had just been cleared of tenants. The whole site and everything it held had long been paid for and its book value was the symbolic DM1. The value of the shed was a fraction of one Deutschmark. Everyone knows how much young people, and many grown men too, who live in apartment houses would love to have a shed: somewhere to repair their mopeds and tinker about. But I don't think that under the present regulations a shed like that could be saved. It would entail maintenance. If anything happened to anyone – who would pay? Who would keep an eye on the young people – they might even make love in there! That's the kind of thing you hear. The housing association is investing here, so bit by bit our hopes for a better way of life fade away.

Individual renovation projects should form the occasion to raise yet again the question of the quality of life in housing, with all the ideas on rented garden plots, hutches for real rabbits, club rooms, common workshops – instead of which it has degenerated into another way of victimising the economically-weakest members of society into paying higher rents; in other words, another way of guaranteeing profits for some big capitalist undertaking. It is for that reason that Hämer has painted the houses he has been able to save from destruction not in the old way but in bright modern colours –they are modern social housing, with modern financing, modern rents and modern profits for those who have provided the credit. If the man in the street could ever really be informed of the financial interests involved, we might perhaps be able to achieve quite a different type of renovation. Why can the long-amortised buildings not be handed over to the tenants? Or taken over by the state?

Of course these are sentimental questions; as if the organisers – the politicians who represent us in parliament, the civil servants who run our cities and our state, the managers of the non-profit housing associations acting in the public interest – as if they could be expected to support the weak and the disadvantaged and provide them with cheap housing. Or give us all a breathing space before the complete takeover by capitalist arithmetic. No, the renovators are left to organise the complete destruction of our cities, to sell the heritage of generations for what they consider a mere pittance and force us to give our lives up to anonymous evaluation pressures. They do not need to fear us: we will certainly never be in a position to take them to task. But not only our children but their children, too, will be threatened by the monotony of the standardised rabbit hutch and the terror of asocial gangs of youths that may threaten their old age as it does ours.

Translated from the German by Eileen Martin

NOTES

1 Before the Fachbereich Architektur of the HfbK Berlin, that of the TH Darmstadt and in public on 29 April 1975 in the Urania, Berlin.
2 Illustrations and ground plan in Erika Schachinger, *Alte Wohnhäuser in Berlin*, Berlin 1969.
3 See Illustration 3 of the essay by Ernst Badstübner in this issue.
4 Illustrated in G Schiedlausky, *Martin Grünberg*, Burg 1942.
5 Illustrated in Schachinger, *op.cit.*
6 Illustrated in Hermann Schmitz, *Berliner Baumeister vom Ausgang des 18 Jahrhunderts*, Berlin 1914. In the following I refer to the facade on p 95.
7 *Technische Deputation für Gewerbe, Grundlage der praktischen Baukunst*, Berlin 1830. This contains a number of Schinkel's designs for houses. The one discussed here is plates 37-39. Schinkel also published this in his collection *Sammlung Architektonischer Entwürfe*, plates 63 and 64, clearly because the publication by the State took so long. His private publication appeared in 1826.
8 There are a number of publications specifically on Luisenstadt and studies in connection with renovation; but so far as I know there is no serious academic study and documentation of what has been and is being destroyed during the renovation.
9 Illustration and ground plan in Fritz Monke, *Grundrissentwicklung und Aussehen des Berliner Miethauses von 1850 bis 1914 dargestellt an Beispielen aus dem Stadtteil Moabit*, Thesis, TU Berlin, 1968.
10 Prenzlauerberg in East Berlin is still more or less intact as urban form, however low the state of the fabric. (Editor's note)
11 Ground plan in *Berlin und sein Bauen*, 1877.
12 Cf Note 8.
13 For a summary see Rudolf Eberstadt, *Handbuch des Wohnungswesens und der Wohnungsfrage*, Jena, 1912.

Klaus Homann and Ludovica Scarpa
Martin Wagner, The Trades Union Movement and Housing Construction in Berlin in the first half of the Nineteen Twenties

Article 155 of the constitution of the German *Reich* stated in 1919 that the new state had 'as its aim the provision of a healthy place to live for every German citizen', and was one of the attempts to reorganise housing construction in Berlin. It was an aim shared by many architects and engineers, particularly those who were Social Democrats. We are limiting ourselves to the work of Martin Wagner during the first half of the Weimar Republic, when he achieved housing of major importance in Berlin, an achievement publicly acknowledged with his election as Civic Councillor for Building in 1926 and hence director of town planning.

When the article was written, the housing shortage in Berlin had reached proportions worse than anything known for a long time. Nothing had been built between 1914 and 1918, and the soldiers returning from the war tended to congregate in the cities; as a result, the number of new families rose. Although the price of land had dropped so low that building was possible, the price of new housing was far above the pre-war level, largely due to the collapse in energy supply and the resultant shortage of tiles and cement.

Housing construction financed only by private funds, as had been the case before the First World War, could not have produced apartments at rents which tenants could have afforded to pay. Nationalisation of production was still under discussion in the years immediately after the war, but in reality the entrepreneurs and the unions had reached agreement over the heads of the workers not to do this (Stinnes-Legien Agreement). The only possibility was to subsidise building costs while maintaining state control of rents – a form of housing control introduced during the war.

The housing shortage, as all concerned knew well, could only be alleviated by producing cheaper housing. Only then would workers, too, be able to afford anything like a decent place to live. But for Wagner, as he wrote as early as 1918, subsidisation was not an actual production of cheaper housing; it was only a re-distribution of the costs. He regarded it as senseless to support the less productive building industry with funds drawn from more productive sectors. Capital should yield a 'normal' return everywhere, and all sectors of the economy should be equally productive. While in reality the trusts and monopolies were making the differences in productivity in different areas and countries throughout the world (profiting with the help of state aid), Wagner was dreaming of an equalisation of productivity, thus hoping to re-establish a liberal, and in this case social, capitalism.

For him, therefore, the rationalisation of production in the building industry was the only meaningful way to provide housing at prices people could afford; any other way was only patchwork and could at best be only a temporary solution. In 1918 he was considering who could finance the rationalisation programme after the war, and his first idea was a working cooperative between industry and the state. After the revolutionary events from November 1918 to January 1919 a new possibility presented itself. The unions and the SPD were

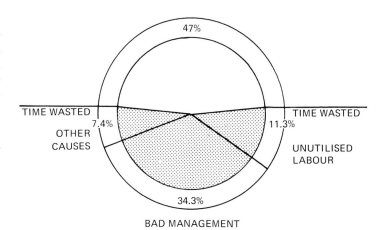

1 Time wasted in the US building industry and its causes as established by an American commission.

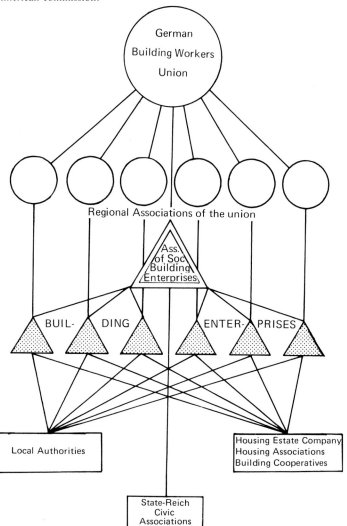

2 Diagram showing the structure of the *Bauhütten*.

58

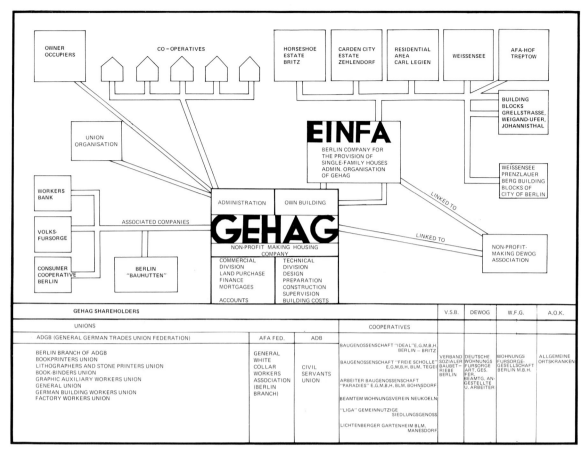

3 Diagram showing the structure of the new association of union enterprises.

under pressure from members demanding practical exercise of new power in the interests of the workers: first and foremost this meant the implementation of socialisation measures. The discussion on how this should be done could not be procrastinated indefinitely, and when Wagner put forward his rationalisation programme with a few additions, describing it as 'the socialisation of building enterprises', it was supported with considerable publicity by the leaders of the building workers union. Wagner wanted to establish enterprises which combined rationalisation with profit restriction and he received from the unions the commission and the money to do so.

His *Bauhütten*, constructed along the lines of British guild socialism, were greeted as a practical step on the road to socialisation. In structure they were deliberately analogous to private capitalist enterprises with which they were to compete with better technology and organisation, and with a further productivity factor: the enthusiasm of the workers for socialism. This would force or persuade private enterprises to reduce their profits, plan their activities and so produce cheaper housing. Shortly after the first *Bauhütte* was founded in Berlin in 1919, Wagner actually challenged the private builders to join the unions in pursuing the aim of rationalisation by cooperating in a research establishment. His offer, however, was ignored. On the contrary, the private builders used their connections with the materials suppliers to put as many obstacles as they could in the path of the 'social building companies', as their new competitors called themselves. They did not hesitate to borrow from the communists for their propaganda against the *Bauhütten*, which had been described by the communist spokesman on housing, Walter Ulbricht, as 'the latest socialisation swindle of the ADGB (General German Trade Unions Federation)'.

The social building companies did not collapse, as the private builders had prophesised, but neither did they take the upswing their founders had envisaged. The cities and local authorities, from whom their main contracts should have come, were often sceptical, if not directly hostile. The continuous flow of orders, which was essential for large-scale purchases of equipment and hence rationalisation, was not achieved. In Berlin the social enterprises put up only a few buildings between 1920 and 1924, such as parts of the Tempelhofer Feld estate and Eichkamp and the ADGB head office.

As the state did not prove a satisfactory means of support for the growth of the social enterprises, Wagner cast around for other means of achieving continuous financing. Again it was the unions which supported his efforts at common enterprise and provided him with funds through the newly established *Arbeiterbank* (Workers' Bank). The *Dewog* (Deutsche Wohnungsfürsorge-Aktiengesellschaft für Beamte, Angestellte und Arbeiter, that is the German Housing Company for Officials, Clerical Workers and Workers) was to use union funds (savings deposited with the Workers' Bank and the state subsidies which had been put on a new basis after the end of inflation) in such a way as to begin the planned construction of 'housing for the lower income groups'. Other companies were founded for the organisation and implementation of the planning and building work, for example the *Neue Heimat* (New Home) in Hamburg and the *Gehag* in Berlin. Their shares were held by some existing cooperatives, the unions, the *Dewog*, the 'Association of Social Building Enterprises' (*Verband sozialer Baubetriebe*) and the civic 'Housing Provision Company' (*Wohnungsfürsorgegesellschaft GmbH*). This put non-nationalised, non-profit housing construction on a new basis under the leadership of the unions.

The new association of union enterprises looked like a well-organised trust, and the unions very proudly characterised it as one. However, the principle of free competition was never abandoned and the *Gehag*, for instance, awarded contracts through the usual tender procedure to private builders as well if their offer was cheaper than that of the social enterprises. The *Gehag* never succeeded in realising planned investment of machinery and factories to bring its prices and costs down over the longer term. It tried to obtain a maximum of the state subsidies – although these came very irregularly – and build with them.

But what was the practical work of building like in the new organisation? The *Gehag* received its first major commission for 1000 apartments, 11% of the total housing production in Berlin for the previous year, which it built to designs by the architects Bruno Taut and Martin Wagner. In the southern district of Berlin, in Britz, the city had released land which had formerly been agricultural for building, and they sold it relatively cheaply. Here the first big estate was built, the Horseshoe estate, which was to make Berlin famous as the centre of *Neues Bauen* (New Building) and as a city with a social housing policy. Planning was for six months ahead and began in May 1925; this enabled some reductions in costs which would not have been possible in smaller projects: the authorities permitted the width of the streets inside the estate to be reduced, which ultimately had a positive effect on the overall production costs. The design costs were minimised because only four types of houses were used. The building work was carried out by the *Bauhütte Berlin* and to a certain extent it proved possible to replace hand work by machines. A bagger was purchased, and transport belt and tracks were laid to remove the soil in the simplest possible way. But the fact that this was a single commission, or at any rate the uncertainty over whether any further contracts would be given, set limits to the investment that was possible in machinery and equipment.

One major contract was not continuity as Wagner had envisaged it. This also affected the purchase of materials, where with tiles, for example, economies of scale would have been possible. Under the prevailing market conditions an integration of tile production and consumption was not possible. Building was still far removed from what was already technically possible and should have been utilised to keep the costs down.

Nevertheless, the big estate was celebrated not only as a step on the way to rationalisation but as a result of rationalisation. Even so, it was only the result of one major contract; the union aim of keeping building costs down had only been achieved to a very minor extent. But the buildings were given a form which was to show what a rationalised estate should look like. Not only this: they were to be a model for a new form of organisation and economy which would give a social turn to capitalism and make socialisation unnecessary: 'the common-weal economy'. These two elements were united in the architectural form as an anticipation and preparation for a new awareness of equality:

'In the south of the city, in Britz, in the estate and elsewhere, the great simple idea of huge masses of people living together is given clear expression: one sees with one's own eyes the power of uniformity, uniformity is given expression as a creed. In the houses in ordinary streets the masses of people were crowded together, cramped, sullied, so to speak, without any sense of identity. Here they have peace and self-awareness. They live separately here too but the great buildings, more knowing than their inhabitants, are a

4 Bagger owned by the *Deutsche Bauhütte* on a building site in Britz. The shovel scrapes away the earth and tips it on to a conveyor belt. The elimination of hand work increases performance sevenfold.

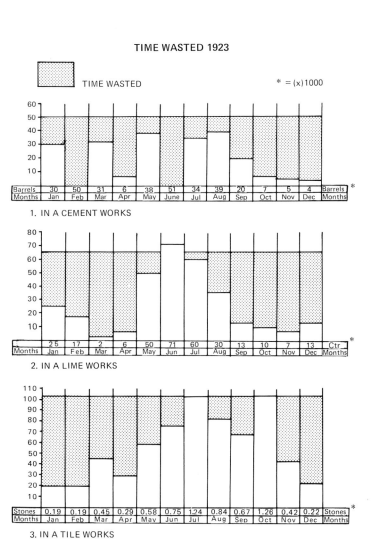

5 Time wasted in the building materials industry.

6 Aerial view of the building site in Britz. Work under the charge of *Gehag*, directed by Dir. Gutschmidt and Linneke, carried out by *Deutsche Bauhütte* under the direction of the Government master builder, Herr A. Hackland.

living expression of what is happening here. It is a long process of education like a silent daily sermon.'[1]

But who was being educated in Britz, in Zehlendorf and the later estates in Berlin, for which the first two remained the model?

Who lived in the big estates?

The conditions of production and financing resulted in rents which working-class families could not afford. They remained behind in the old tenements, in their overcrowded apartments with a parlour and a kitchen. The people who moved out of the city to the new estates (apart from highly-paid skilled workers, civil servants and the self-employed) were mainly white-collar workers, a class between the bourgeoisie and the proletariat which only fully developed under the changing conditions in production and organisation in the nineteen twenties. Their growing numbers and political uncertainty meant that under parliamentary conditions they could be a decisive factor in the success or failure of any government coalition. It was hardly by accident that they were a main focus of attention for the social democrat reformers. So a solution to the housing problem, promised to every German in the constitution of Weimar, was only achieved for the white-collar workers and even then only for some.

Creating decent human conditions for the workers would have entailed different economic conditions and a different policy. Perhaps many of the proposals of Martin Wagner might then have been realised. As it was, they remained unrealised ideas and an ideal, which in only one exceptional case was given visible manifestation in building.

Translated from the German by Eileen Martin

Ludovica Scarpa
Born in Venice 1955. Studied history of architecture in the Departimento di Analisi Critica e Storica at the Instituto Universitario de Architettura di Venezia. Prepared a thesis about Martin Wagner and Berlin with Prof. Manfredo Tafuri and Prof. Marco De Michelis. Prepared a special issue for the architectural magazine Rassegna, Problemi di Architettura dell' Ambiente *on Technik in the Twenties in Europe which appeared December 1980. Is a scientific collaborator of the Departimento di Analisi Critica e Storica of the IUAV, Venice, where he takes part in historical research about the twenties and thirties in Europe.*

Klaus Homann
Born in 1945. From 1969 to 1970 worked as an assistant director in theatre and television. Studied architecture at the Technical University, Berlin. Between 1978 and 1979 worked on the collection of images and documents related to the work of Martin Wagner; also worked on the essays of Wagner published between 1909 and 1957 (approximately 500) for the Academie Der Künste, Berlin. This work should be seen as preparation for an exhibition planned for 1985. At present is working on a research project concerning the history of the Berlin 'Mietshaus' during the years 1862 to 1930 together with three other architectural historians. The first part of the work has been recently published (J.F. Geist and K. Kürvers, Das Berliner Mietshaus 1740-1862, *München 1980).*

Note
1 Alfred Döblin from *Introduction to Berlin*, book of photographs by Mario V. Bucovich, Berlin, 1928.

1 View from the garden, 1977.

2 View from the street, 1977.

Dietrich von Beulwitz
The Perls House by Ludwig Mies van der Rohe

The Occasion

Anyone who combed through the villa areas of Berlin at the beginning of the new building boom in 1977 in search of a plot of land or a 'country house complex with commercial premises' would have found a rather dubious object turning up in the estate agents' offers month after month.

On the very edge of the Grunewald, the property offered 'Possibility of conversion into owner-occupier apartments' or 'Building land with buildings to be demolished' and anyone who was interested enough to go and look found himself wandering through a maze of suburban office buildings (dating from about 1950), an undatable confusion of barracks with some Neoclassical details on the cornices and the fragment of a villa, of a strange severity, almost hidden by all this. The property and site had once been used by a commercial enterprise which produced medical and technical apparatus and, it was known, had done something similar during the war, designing measuring instruments for jet aircraft and V-weapons.

No-one could find a use for all this. Thank heavens for that: for the core of the little factory, the fragment of a villa almost hidden with ivy was indeed the Perls house dating from 1911, almost totally forgotten; it was the second building which Mies van der Rohe designed alone, together with an extension he planned in 1928. The records give the architect's name as Göbbels. But Mies van der Rohe, who was then still working in Peter Behrens' studio, had formed an association with Göbbels and acknowledges the house as his.

The Building

It is a two-storey plastered brick building. The flat hipped roof, covered with pantiles, only begins above a cornice which concludes the building. The ground plan was strictly axial before the alterations, with slight functional interruptions. The asymmetrical entrance to the street is reached through a front garden which is set slightly below street level. The square hall leads to the main room on the ground floor, the library and the stairs. The ground floor is only one step above the level of the garden and the main room was originally reached from the garden through a deep-set loggia. All the interior arrangements – the official rooms downstairs leading into the garden through closely-set French floor-to-ceiling windows, the more intimate rooms upstairs – have that spaciousness and care which make Mies' Neoclassical architecture a legitimate part of his work as a whole. When I was finally entrusted by the Historical Preservation Office with the restoration of the villa – an institution had come forward which could make use of the property and promised to treat the valuable substance with the appropriate care – I found myself delving into a stirring chapter of twentieth-century history.

The Protagonists

The people who give the Perls House its exemplary significance could have come out of a contemporary play by Rolf Hochhuth: the contractor, Hugo Perls, a wealthy bourgeois art dealer and legal expert in the Ministry for Foreign Affairs; his friends, Karl Liebknecht, a Communist member of the Reichstag; the architect, Mies van der Rohe; the painter, Max Pechstein; the art historian, collector and Socialist Eduard Fuchs, second owner and the man who commissioned the extension. Then the historical break: murder, flight, emigration of the righteous, the removal of the art treasures from the house by the SS, the house left for years to stand empty and decay, then occupied and its original character destroyed by the unpolitical scientist from the Kaiser-Wilhelm-Institut, a colleague of Max Planck's with a flair for business, a designer of measuring instruments for new weapons under the special protection of Speer. The house becomes a laboratory and an armaments project, its seclusion a security asset. Nineteen-forty-five: the zero hour? Not for this firm, whose real prosperity only now begins, with different products. Our drama closes, on a quiet note, when the company, which is bursting at the seams, moves out.

Reconstruction

The work of restoration begins. Measuring, carefully removing the encrustations and distortions, layer by layer. First of all a study of the plans in the building records, but these are incomplete and confusing. The search for the original, almost lost beneath the many additions and alterations. Questions. But who can I ask? The widow of the man who founded the company and her photographs. An autobiographical publication by Perls. A visit by Philip Johnson, who shows me his photographs. The Mies van der Rohe Archive in the Museum of Modern Art, but this is unsatisfactory. Sergius Ruegenberg, former colleague of Mies. And back, again and again, to the archaeologist's little hammer.

It proves particularly difficult to restore the original state of the facade, as modern plaster and paint, all industrial products, are quite different from the old materials. Some of the firms commissioned to restore the house decline to take responsibility, arguing that what they are being asked to do is not the proper way to handle modern materials; for instance, a cornice without a protective metal lathe or an injection base only 10cm high or plastering straight on to wood. On the other hand, no one was in a position to use the old materials, eg plaster of slaked lime or horse-hair lime mortar where there is particular exposure. Or a lime paint put on 'al fresco' and combining with the plaster, rubbing off slightly over the course of time and giving a particularly lively effect. These examples could be multiplied. Compromises had to be made, which only the practised eye can recognise now. The paint we finally used is what is known as 'Keim mineral paint'. This also combines with the plaster but it does not rub off. Not to be able to restore the original interior was a particular loss, but the use to which the house is now to be put, as a home for handicapped children, hardly made that possible.

But let us go back to the beginning of our story: Hugo Perls,

3 Reconstruction plans, 1978.

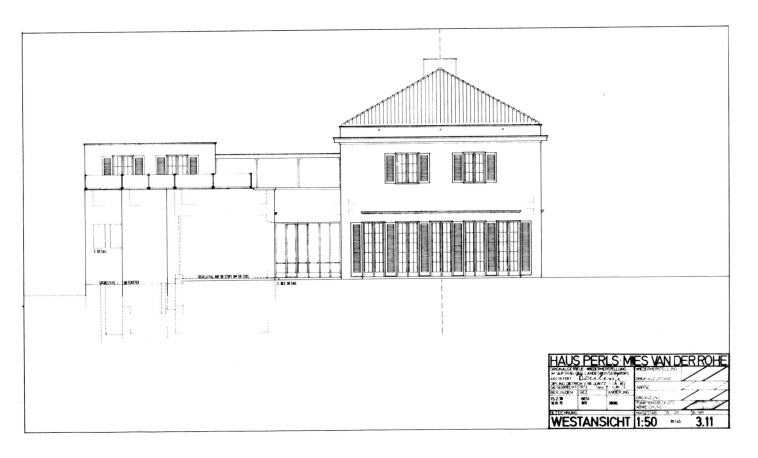

HAUS PERLS · MIES VAN DER ROHE

ORIGINALGETREUE WIEDERHERSTELLUNG IM AUFTRAG DES LANDESKONSERVATORS		WIEDERHERSTELLUNG
ARCHITEKT *Berlin*		ORIGINALZUSTAND
DIPL.ING. DIETRICH v. BEULWITZ · B.D.A · A.I.V GESEBRECHTSTR'3 · 1000 B· KLIN '12		ABRISZ
BERLIN DEN	GEZ	ÄNDERUNG
15.2.78 18.10.79	BEU DER	SOCKEL
BEZEICHNUNG		MASZSTAB B. GR. BL. NR
WESTANSICHT	1:50	81/45 3.11

S DETAIL

SOCKELFUGE : DIE FENSTER

SOCKELFUG. AUF DIE STUFE UM DIE ECKE

S MES DETAIL

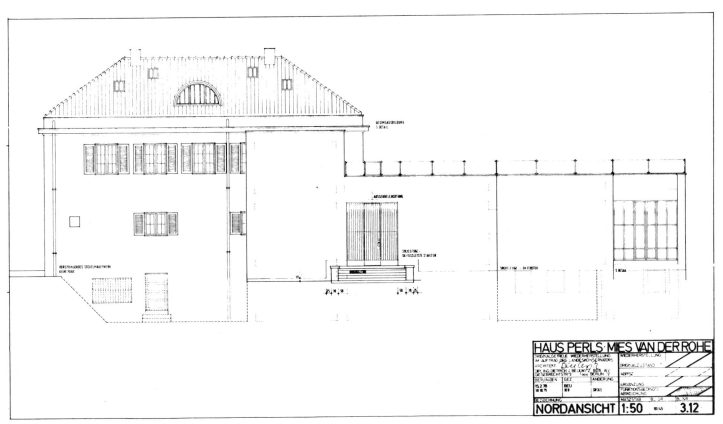

GESIMSAUSBILDUNG S DETAIL

AUSSENBELEUCHTUNG

SOCKELFUGE : DIE FUSSLEISTE STAHLTÜR

VORSPRINGENDES SOCKELMAUERWERK KEINE FUGE

SOCKELFUGE : DIE FENSTER

S DETAIL

HAUS PERLS · MIES VAN DER ROHE

ORIGINALGETREUE WIEDERHERSTELLUNG IM AUFTRAG DES LANDESKONSERVATORS		WIEDERHERSTELLUNG
ARCHITEKT *Berlin*		ORIGINALZUSTAND
DIPL.ING. DIETRICH J. BEULWITZ · BDA · A.IV GESEBRECHTSTR'3 · 1000 BERLIN '12		ABRISZ
BERLIN DEN	GEZ	ÄNDERUNG
15.2.78 18.10.79	BEU DER	SOCKEL
BEZEICHNUNG		MASZSTAB B. GR. BL. NR
NORDANSICHT	1:50	81/45 3.12

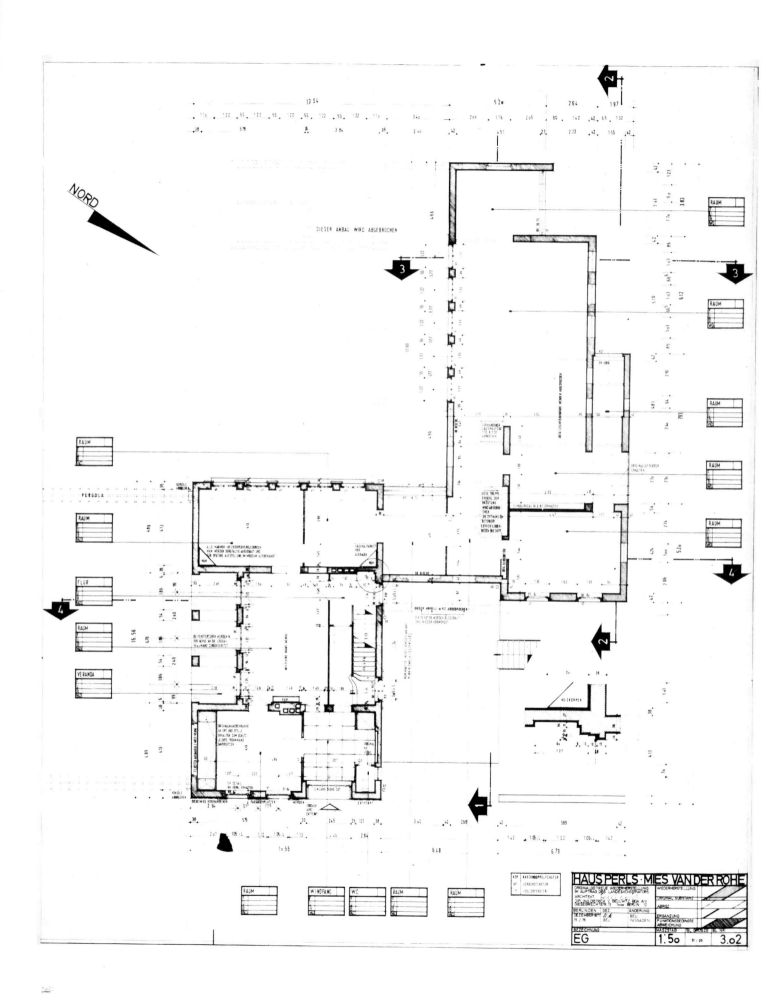

4,5 Wall decoration in the dining room, oil paintings on canvas by Max Pechstein.

the owner, wrote in his memoirs:

'So one evening Ludwig Mies van der Rohe came. He and I were of the same age, he had been born in Aachen and his mother, I think, the other side of the border in Holland. Van der Rohe did not say much but the few things he did say made a deep impression on me. In building something like a new era seemed to have begun. The better architects were concerned to keep superfluous decoration, nooks and crannies, projections and all the appurtenances of romanticism off their facades. a new classicism was coming into being, people were beginning to talk about "dignity" in architecture – after all, van der Velde had introduced morality into architecture. What was being built today was at least rather less terrible than the generally showy architecture of the Wilhelmine period. Van der Rohe held some strong convictions. If I remember rightly, he put his views on the way a house should come into being rather like this: the architect should get to know the people who are going to live in the house. From their needs and requirements all the rest would follow naturally. Of course the position, the direction the house is to face and the size of the land would play an important part, as well as the wishes of the contractor, in determining the ultimate ground plan. All these factors together would organically result in the "where" and "how" of the exterior. He was already talking about the functions of the different parts of the house but the rather dogmatic word "functionalism" was not then in use, I think.

'Mies van der Rohe would have nothing to do with traditional forms. But that did not prevent him appreciating them in the architecture of the past. And so we met in our delight in Schinkel. I see Schinkel as a unique phenomenon; I do not believe that any architect before or after has had his ability to design in the "Gothic" tradition one day and in the "Greek" the next without ever losing his originality.

'In the Grunewald, near Krumme Lanke, Mies van der Rohe built our house. My far too conservative ideas led to many a friendly skirmish. The house could have been better, for Mies was one of the founders of the new architecture. Only a few years later he produced his design for a tower block in iron and cement, as he was to build 30 years later in Chicago and 40 years later in New York. He was so far in advance of his time.'

The Historical Sequence

Although Hugo Perls accuses himself of being too conservative in his ideas on architecture, the meeting of the two in the late summer of 1910 must be seen as a particularly fortunate occurrence compared with two other commissions Mies received at this period, the neighbouring Werner house and the much-publicised Villa Urbig. The Perls house, fruit of his decisive period in Peter Behrens' studio, is the first to document the influence of Schinkel. The strong Neoclassical impulses which he received during this period go on – although this is not generally recognised – into the twenties: witness the Urbig house of 1914, the Eichstaed house of 1921-22. What all three have in common, apart from their clear axial construction, is the flat sloping roof so beloved by Schinkel, the projecting cornice and the wide opening of the garden storey, either through a loggia or the characteristic French windows (also evident in the work of Peter Behrens). There is a further influence which is very apparent. When Mies came to Berlin from Aachen in 1905, he worked for two years with Bruno Paul, the well-known furniture and interior designer, who has also left us some excellent houses in the Neoclassical style. The Auerbach house of 1924-25 shows this very clearly, despite the expressionist influence in some of its details.

Perls also engaged Max Pechstein to work on the interior of the house:

'Max Pechstein had decorated the dining-room in the house Mies van der Rohe designed. He produced 38 nudes, all in ochre, green and blue on white grounds. Later I gave the paintings, which were on canvas, to Justi for his 50th birthday. He built a fine room for them in the Nationalgalerie but they disappeared soon after and I do not know what happened to them.'

Pechstein also designed the metal screens for the radiators on the ground floor. But the freestone details on the screens clearly show Mies' hand, anticipating his famous exterior corners on the Illinois Institute of Technology building (the drawings of which are now in the Werkbundarchiv in Berlin).

The Radicals

Now to Karl Liebknecht, of whom Perls writes:

6 Radiator screen, dining-room.

7 Radiator screen, salon.

'Liebknecht was a very unusual man, he seemed the incarnation of Socialism. Martin Luther was one of his ancestors and he resembled him in his love of conflict. He had wavy black hair, black fiery eyes, an expression of energy and confidence, and yet a certain fear that things might not work out seemed to mingle with this. The fine bronze bust which the British sculptor Jacob Epstein made of him will show what I mean.

'We left the banker and sat on this first evening of our acquaintance until far into the summer night in our garden. "Look", he soon said, "your pictures are all very well, but what use are they? Nude men and women, portraits of young people who have done nothing for the movement and then the Eiffel tower! Believe me, the great painter was Courbet – not his waves and woods but everything he did while he was concerned with the social philosophy of his friend Proudhon. That is art that can be used to some good. Your architect seems a very capable man. Wait till the Independent Socialists are in power and we'll be able to make good use of him.'

The fate of Liebknecht did indeed occupy Mies but in a way that could hardly be foreseen at the time!

'The "bourgeois" Social Democrats now became Liebknecht's greatest enemies. From then on his life was constantly in danger. Once I succeeded in warning him. It was in December 1918, I was still working in the Ministry for Foreign Affairs and heard five young attachés outside in the corridor discussing what they were planning to do. Liebknecht was to speak that evening in Hasenhaide, they were drawing lots as to who should do the deed. I went to a telephone and warned him. The meeting was held an hour earlier than planned and the assassins came too late. But my other warnings of a more general kind were of no avail. "My place is on the barricades". The rest is history. The finest monument of our time, designed by Mies van der Rohe and commissioned by four of Liebknecht's friends, was destroyed by the vandals of the Thousand Year Reich.'

This might lead people to think that the post-war European avant-garde in architecture, and hence Mies too, were close to Socialist groups. But the social engagement of the radical Berlin architects, with the exception of Bruno Taut and Hannes Mayer, was not of very great importance. In comparison to the Russian avant-garde, they were unpolitical and tended to a bourgeois elitism (that is true of Mendelsohn, Gropius and the Luckhard brothers).* So, as D.D. Egbert tells us in *Social Radicalism*, the commission to design the monument to Karl Liebknecht was given rather by chance to Mies:

'To the author Mies wrote concerning that monument: "Everything was accidental from the beginning to the end. But let me tell you the facts.

"One of the first houses I built was for Hugo Perls in Berlin. Mr. Perls sold his house in the early twenties to a Mr. Eduard Fuchs. Mr. Fuchs had a huge collection of Daumiers and other artists. He told friends of mine he would like to build a wing on to his house as a gallery for his collection and for this he would like to talk to me. A few days later a friend of mine told me he was going to Mr. Fuchs for dinner. I asked him if it would not be an opportune time for me to meet Mr. Fuchs. This meeting was arranged.

"After discussing his house problems Mr. Fuchs then said he wanted to show us something. This turned out to be a photograph of a model for a monument to Karl Liebknecht and Rosa Luxemburg. [Both, as leaders of the extreme left Spartakusbund were murdered in Berlin, 1919.] It was a huge stone monument with Doric columns and medallions of Luxemburg and Liebknecht. When I saw it I started to laugh and told him it would be a fine monument for a banker.

"He must have been very much disturbed by this remark because the next morning he called me and said that as I had laughed at the monument he had shown he would like to know what I would propose. I told him I hadn't the slightest idea what I would do in his place but as most of these people were shot in front of a wall, a brick wall would be what I would build as a monument. Fuchs could not imagine how a brick wall could be used as a monument but told me that if I had an idea he would be interested in seeing it. A few days later I showed him my sketch of the monument which in the end was built.

"He was still sceptical about it and particularly when I showed him the bricks I would like to use. In fact he had the greatest trouble to gain permission from his friends who were to build the monument.'"

*Editor's note:
An exception should be made for the short period after the war, when socialist ideas had been discussed (for example, in the Novembergruppe).

New Contractors

The highly-cultured Eduard Fuchs would certainly have intervened among his friends in the Communist party. His collection of erotic and satirical art and caricatures was then unique and his publications had made him famous as the 'Zittenfuchs' (Moral Fox)§. Politically he was party treasurer to the Communist party. Reidemeister, the art historian, tells us how Fuchs could have been seen in the 1920s, an elegantly-clad gentleman, always in spats, in the S-Bahn on the way from the rich villa colony in Zehlendorf to a party meeting in the centre of the city. Hugo Perls has this to say about his successor in the house:

'The "Moral Fox" had begun to take an interest in Daumier at an early age and he needed illustrations for the many and attractive books he wrote for Albert Langen in Munich. So he often went to Paris, where he could find what he wanted. He walked around the "quais", first buying a few dozen lithographs by Daumier and later thousands of them. He showed a dozen to Max Liebermann and got his first picture. This went on until he had 15 pictures by Liebermann. Then he took five of these and asked me if I would give him my house for them. I agreed, for a house without cosy corners was hardly saleable on the open market. The Liebermanns brought in so much money that the house was fully paid for, and Mies van der Rohe could have been content, for Fuchs' collections soon grew to such a degree that two annexes [it was only one: author] were needed, which he was commissioned to build . . . Do I need to say that Fuchs, who loved figures, did all the calculations for me! Certainly he was one of the very small group of real patrons of the arts.

'After he had given up his dangerous journalism and devoted himself entirely to writing books he soon began to earn a great deal of money, which he invested in Daumiers and Slevogts. He was very modest in his own needs. Before moving into my house he had lived in a few attic rooms, something between Spitzweg's "Impoverished Poet" and Daumier's "Amateur d'Estampes".'

§Editor's note:
'Zitten' : good manners in the erotic sense

8 Laboratory workers have a tea-break, 1940.

9 The 'Economic Miracle' behind the extension, 1977.

10 The main house, 1977.

Elsewhere Perls describes how friends of Fuchs' from Brünn were delighted with the house and asked who the architect was. They met Mies in Hermannstrasse and he made a design for them, quite different from the Perls house, causing great surprise. But finally they did decide to give him the contract. Their name was Tugendhat.

The extension needed to the Perls house in 1928 faced Mies with the delicate task of on the one hand not betraying his new views on architecture and on the other of remaining true to the old Neoclassical building. He did not hesitate to build an extension on two storeys to the old house and, apart from the French windows to the common courtyard and the projection to redirect rainwater, introduced new elements: the emphasis on certain sections of the wall outside and inside, the gradation of certain elements, the flat roof (which was still causing him a lot of trouble at that time). Unaware of the problems (the technology was not yet available), he decided in favour of large welded asphalt sheets and a very thick layer of plates on a peat base. After a short time the plates stretched and split and the rain came in on Fuchs' costly collection – drawings, books, old Chinese sculptures. Fuchs was beside himself with anger and Mies had to find a new roofing; this time he used a highly-praised American product but even this only survived Fuchs' residency in the house for a short time.

As was characteristic of Fuchs and his relations with his 'business partners', Mies, like Perls before him, had to take payment in kind, at any rate for the design of the monument: this time it was a six-volume edition of Fuchs' main work, *The History of Erotic Art*.

In 1932 Philip Johnson, who was then working on his book on Schinkel's pupils, Persius and Stühler, stayed in the Perls house together with Mies. He still remembers the strong 'Schinkel ochre' in which both parts of the house were painted, and particularly his delight in the new way Mies had designed the grilles in front of the windows of the extension. The photos which were of such value to me, however, were not taken until later, probably in 1936. Fuchs had had to leave Germany as fast as he could. Perls:

'The Nazis emptied his house. They needed several lorries to take away the 20,000 copper engravings, the 10,000 books and hundreds of paintings and sculptures and store them for the Reich of the Great Illusion. In Paris Fuchs was overcome by fear. So as not to be recognised he grew a fine beard which really made him look like a Socialist. But it wasn't necessary; no-one touched him and he certainly did no-one any harm. He had a great love of mankind and was a true and faithful friend. In any case his Socialism waned remarkably in Paris.'

The New Era

So the house stood empty. The new owners, when they came, could not adjust to the design of the house. Their work was so utterly different. The widow of the head of the firm said, looking back, 'We had to turn it into a proper house.' Heaven knows, they did a thorough job, as might be expected of German scientists from the Kaiser-Wilhelm-Institut (it is the Max-Planck Institute now). They turned everything upside down: the loggia was closed, the terraced roof built over, the courtyard which had been created by the extension roofed over to form a factory. They put air-raid shelters in the garden, built walks connecting the house with two neighbouring villas and disguised them as pergolas, and as time went on they altered more and more of Mies' facade, putting in different windows, chipping off the frieze, making the entrance more 'representative' with travertine and aluminium. In the old and the new cellars they worked away like moles, measuring, researching, producing their stuff. 'The German spirit of invention' was hard at it. The original architect, of course, was written off as utterly useless. He couldn't even construct a proper flat roof!

The Economic Miracle

The competent planning authorities subsequently approved the building sins committed in the war without worrying about the old property. Production is more important than any 'questionable' architecture; anything which could bring investment has to be utilised. Even now, after the restoration of the exterior, the house is still caught between a new aggressive use and the claims of history. Let's meet here again in sixty years' time.

11-13 View from the street, the loggia and extension after restoration.

Benjamin Warner
Berlin – The Nordic Homeland and the Corruption of Urban Spectacle

The Transition to Fascism

In 1933, at the culmination of a series of electoral results disastrous for the German democratic parties, the German Nazi Party under the leadership of Adolf Hitler assumed control of the State and later that year gained a sizeable majority in the Reichstag. The Weimar government of the previous fourteen years had been unable to stimulate enthusiasm for social democracy among the German people nor, in the face of considerable economic distress, to bring convincing personalities to the forefront of German politics. Ten years after Hitler's unsuccessful 'putsch' of 1923, the promises of political and economic reform, together with a 'German cultural "renaissance"', appeared to be within the grasp of the German people. Berlin, which since the early nineteen-twenties was seen by the German provinces as a symbol of decadence and Bolshevism, was to be purged. Three years later, in 1936, oppression of individual life and the hysterical glorification of leadership became outward signs of a society whose dreams of 1933, however difficult to comprehend, had been distorted by the cynicism of an authoritarian regime.

The Nordic Homeland

The means by which the Nazi party won public sympathy still inspires much discussion among those who study ideology and participation in politics. Erich Fromm, for example, has written about Hitler's exploitations of the sado-masochistic weaknesses in the German personality.[1] His writings echo those

1 *Capital City* by Otto Dix. The 'decadence' of Weimar Germany which the fascists wished to remove.

2 Communist Party election poster from 1929. They too wished to remove 'decadence' and 'corruption' from German life.

of the French psychologist, Gustav Le Bon, who, in 1922, questioned human rationality in a complex industrialised society.[2] In such a society, powerlessness and rootlessness, it is argued, are said to encourage individual alienation. Fromm, unlike Le Bon, drew on what was to be learnt from the rise of German fascism and notes that both the historical events and the social unrest following the First World War facilitated Hitler's rise to power.[3] These criteria became important in the exploitation of personal insecurity through Nazi ideology, itself a mixture of two paranoic responses; sadistic and masochistic reactions to failure and defeat in the First World War. These two factors recur throughout *Mein Kampf*,[4] sadism acting as the 'unrestricted power over another person more or less mixed with destructiveness and maschochism... aiming at dissolving oneself in an overwhelmingly strong power and participating in strength and glory'.[5] The disillusioned groups to whom Nazi ideology most strongly appealed gladly accepted obedience to a leader and participated in the persecution of racial, political and cultural minorities. They firmly believed in the regime's craving for conquest and the ideology's exaltations of the German people and the Nordic race.

3 *Volkhalle*: the symbolism of such a space clearly evokes the role of the parish church.

Nazism—the Arts and Architecture

To the Nazi party, the arts were always considered of special importance. 'In art, the highest value of the personality will once again assert itself.' The task of art in the Third Reich was to represent 'Nordic man' in all his 'warlike glory with his Nordic homeland in the background'.[6] The nineteen-twenties had seen the rise of so-called 'decadent art' which in architecture was manifest in the works of men such as Bruno Taut, Walter Gropius, Ernst May and Mies van der Rohe.[7] Since the Modern Movement was clearly at odds with the essence of Nazism, it was branded as 'sub-human, a Jewish Bolshevik invention aiming at the destruction of the Nordic

spirit'.[8] This type of criticism was not only levelled at the visual arts but can be found in almost all contemporary literature dealing with the decay of 'German' culture where 'foreign' influences were seen to be corroding the very roots of traditional 'German' society. This could be seen most clearly in the modern city where industrialisation and urban 'sprawl' during the early twentieth century had taken its toll of the image of the traditional German town. An article entitled 'News from the Asphalt Deserts' described the city as 'the melting pot of all evil, of prostitution... Marxism, Jews... negro dancers and all the disgusting offspring of so-called modern art'.[9]

Whilst this type of Nazi propaganda presented and highlighted the less desirable elements of modern culture, those associated to some extent justifiably with the Weimar republic, the attitudes towards the ultimate development of the city under Nazi patronage were contradictory. Ideologists of the nineteen-thirties, men such as Schulz-Naumberg (1869-1949) and Alfred Rosenberg (1893-1946), were both exponents of the *Völkische*[10] theories regarding art and architecture. Schulz-Naumberg described the city as 'the moloch of our time', whilst Alfred Rosenberg's enormously popular book *Myth of the 20th Century*, based on Walter Darré's hypothesis of the interdependence of soil and human organism (*blut und boden*, blood and soil), called for a greater agrarian outlook. Darré himself traced the origins of the German people in his book *The Peasantry as the Life Source of the Nordic Race* and declared that 'Whoever would create a nobility in the genuine and particularly German sense of the word must extract selected families for this purpose out of the city, transplant them into the land and, above all, in conditions under which they can strike roots'.[12]

The city of Berlin, which had been particularly affected by industrialisation and rapid development after 1971, was to be re-instated as a beautiful European city to surpass Vienna or even Paris. It was to be endowed with impressive Neoclassical monuments reflecting the 'greatness and wealth of the community'. As Robert Taylor points out, there lay behind Hitler's ideological view of the city a fundamental reason: his desire for impressive, austere monuments to be seen by the world. The city held the cornerstone of Hitler's power –thousands of people who could be gathered into crowds for his glorification.[13]

It has often been pointed out that the psychology of Nazism was one of preparation for war, 'its success was dependent on the maintenance of a national spirit which in the end must find expression in aggressive action'.[14] Thus urban rituals, although a by-product of Hitler's main aim, were particularly important in instilling this sense of aggressive unity into the masses, a means by which Hitler could realise his international expansionist policies. Although the great spectacles are most popularly associated with aggressive ritual, with their dramatically-staged special effects to intensify 'communal' expression, the appropriation of urban space by the Nazi leaders to form the political mass, demonstrates how crowds were considered a living part of architecture.

The Third Reich provided many 'stages' for this variety of political spectacle. The *Volkhalle* (People's Hall) was common in most towns and cities in the party's formative days. More significant than the hall, however, was the urban square which allowed more room for 'participation'; huge crowds also forced reluctant 'non-believers' to take part.[15] (One can associate this view with, for instance, Mussolini's remodelling of the Piazza Venezia in Rome.)

4 Berlin from the north, the north-south axis by Albert Speer. Flanked with monumentally-scaled classical buildings and with a huge triumphal arch, it expresses a grandiose militarism which would culminate in war.

5 Berlin from the south, the north-south axis.

To a totalitarian state, the creation of an urban scenario encouraging communal submission is of particular importance; but in nineteen-thirties Germany, it is in Berlin, the seat of Government for the 'millenial' Reich, that we can see most clearly the grandiose vision of what might have been. The population of Berlin, which in 1871 had been 800,000, had risen to over four million by 1937. The years following the First World War saw the construction of large housing estates to accommodate the influx of workers. Factories, department stores and all the other trappings of an industrialised society so deplored by right-wing critics had become the norm. This erosion of traditional 'German' culture was seen to be a conscious effort on the part of the European powers to strip Germany of her dignity and status. More specifically, Germany felt threatened from the East and this paranoid fear, true or false, discerned eastern beliefs infiltrating the roots of German culture, hence the much-used expression, *Kulturbolshewismus*. The large housing estates springing up on the outskirts of the larger cities were seen to be the work of Communist collaborators seeking to level off the natural social hierarchy. Every effort was made to discredit the authors of anything which could be said to be Marxist or Bolshevist, and the unfortunate terms of the Modern Movement architects such as 'international' and 'collectivism' did nothing to avert the final tragedy.[16]

Although Berlin contained many fine examples of eighteenth- and nineteenth-century architecture, the Industrial Revolution had transformed it into a 'modern' city. Under its new masters, however, Berlin would assume an identity reflecting Germany's status as an international power. The new city would instil a sense of 'community' into its inhabitants and clearly speak the truths of Nazi ideology by means of its fabric; it would, as Hitler put it, become the 'word in stone'.[17]

Hitler as a young man in Vienna had unsuccessfully attempted to enter the Vienna Academy of Fine Arts to study architecture and had always maintained a strong interest in building. It is possible that Gottfried Von Semper's book, *Uber Baustyle*, which maintained that monumental architecture aided those in power to control the 'apathetic and restless masses', influenced his tastes for the monumental – the main architectural characteristic of the Third Reich. Consistent with Hitler's preference for this style, Neoclassicism was favoured by many critics of the day. It could be said to be of 'Nordic' origin and would moreover point to the kinship of latter-day Germany to the avowed perfection of Ancient Greece. It was also maintained that the classical style would act as a counterweight to the tendency of the 'Aryan' mind to become abstract and 'alien to reality'. Lotz, chairman of the arts section at the Ministry of Education, wrote that it was to be expected that the desired renaissance in the Greek way should include building as the Greeks once did. It was this resultant pared-down, Doric-ordered classical style, then, that was to become the predominant building form in the new Berlin.

In 1937, Albert Speer, a young architect who had come to

6 The Domed Hall, Berlin, by Albert Speer: 'shattering all existing senses of proportion'.

Hitler's attention through his work in organising and decorating party rallies, was appointed General Building Inspector (*Generalbau-inspektor*) for Berlin with unprecedented powers over the city's development. Under the supervision of Hitler, he prepared plans for the restructuring of the city and in June 1938, building work commenced. Little of what Speer conceived was built in the short time remaining before the war, yet his plans give us an idea of the extraordinary intentions of Germany's rulers.

Although Speer was essentially responsible for the new Berlin, he constantly referred to Hitler's predilection for a north-south avenue, inspired by the Champs-Élysées. Together with the east-west axis, this avenue was to connect with four concentric ring roads. The remnants of this intersection still remain in West Berlin guarded by Soviet troops, the most Western presence of the Soviet role in Germany. Taylor points out that these two avenues no doubt satisfied Hitler's desire for 'spacious vistas of impressive monuments' as well as parade avenues and large squares. The north-south axis, itself three miles long and some 150 yards wide, would be much longer than the impressive Unter der Linden part of the east-west axis, and would be the commercial and social centre of the new Reich. It was to be flanked with Neoclassical buildings, ministries interspersed with leisure zones. Speer remarks that Hitler showed little interest in the residential areas of the new city, but confined himself to those buildings and monuments which would impress foreign dignitaries. At the south end of the avenue would rise the new railway terminus linking the centre of Berlin to the provinces of the empire, whilst the existing architectural proportions of Berlin would have been completely shattered by a building which Hitler envisaged at the northern end. Here was to be situated the Great Domed Hall, into which St Peter's Cathedral in Rome could have fitted several times over, a building which Hitler had dreamed of and sketched as early as 1925. This structure, the largest assembly hall ever planned at the time, would have held between 150,000 and 180,000 standing people. In reality the Domed Hall was a great *Volkhalle* intended for communal gatherings. Speer writes that although Hitler had little sympathy for the mystical notions of Rosenberg and Himmler, the hall was essentially a place of worship which would in the course of centuries,

through 'tradition and venerability...acquire an importance to that which St Peter's in Rome has for Catholic Christendom'.[18]

The great hall was to be surrounded on three sides by artificial lakes, necessitating the widening of the River Spree, whilst on the fourth side the great Plaza was to be situated: the Adolf Hitler Platz, large enough to contain one million standing people. The Zeppelin field in Nuremburg was built to hold 240,000 people but this proposed Berlin Platz would be capable of holding four times as many; it was perhaps the most ambitious urban space planned by the regime, one that would make st Peter's Square small by comparison. The May 1st rallies, traditionally held in the Tempelhof field on the outskirts of Berlin, would henceforth be held here. On one side of the Adolf Hitler Platz the new High Command of the armed forces was to be built and facing it, the new Reich chancellery, even greater than the one that was under construction on Voss Strasse. The fourth side was to remain open, permitting a clear view down the north-south axis, through Hitler's 'Triumphal Arch' to the railway terminus at the far end. The political implications of such a plan speak for themselves. Speer wri᠁ : in retrospect that 'while continually proclaiming his |Hitler's| desire for international reconciliation, he was planning buildings of an imperial majesty which could only be won by war.' It was indeed to this end that the whole of the national, political, economic and cultural effort of the nineteen-thirties was directed and such ambitions met little resistance among the German people at the time.

Speer's plans give us a revealing insight into the importance Hitler placed on public buildings both as international showpieces and as theatrical sets for the enactment of public display. A large amount of publicity surrounded the unveiling of the city's plans and it was made quite clear that the new Berlin symbolised a cultural renaissance: 'the planned improvement of several large cities of the Reich is outward proof of this great epoch of our Volk's resurrection'.[20]

This importance placed on the public buildings can be no better demonstrated than by looking at the relative sums of money spent on the building programme. Whereas in 1929, 33% of the total expenditure had been spent on public buildings, this figure had reached 67.5% by 1936, 72.6% in 1937 and 80% by 1938. The war years saw almost 100% of available funds being spent on public buildings.[21] Whereas many private architects were being forced out of business due to lack of work, Hitler was making special arrangements with the Reichsbank to place unlimited sums of money at the disposal of his public sector architects.

Although the plans for the city of Berlin, through their stark monumentalism, 'soldierly discipline' and their unprecedented desire to create long vistas and vast assembly squares, sought to encourage discipline in the city's inhabitants and, moreover, to remind them of their 'heroic' past through 'heroic' scale, let us now consider the phenomena of Nazi ritual. This is perhaps best considered outside the confines of Berlin itself, but quite clearly such ritual was intended everywhere to enhance community experience by means of the mass rally.

Although Nuremberg was considered the city of party rallies, the May 1st celebrations for the day of national labour were traditionally held in Berlin. The first of these occurred in Berlin on the Tempelhof field and Speer was commissioned to design the decorations. Speer wrote that since the *Völk* were now the 'living bone of the state', it therefore required a space in which it could become a 'visible force'. To achieve this, he maintained that the *Völk* needed a 'visible focus' which the

7 Nazi Rally. Podium provides a 'visible focus' whilst temporary decorations such as flag tribunes provide colour and excitement.

8 Rally in Zeppelin field in Nuremberg organised by Speer. 'Like being inside a cathedral of ice', said Sir Neville Henderson.

9 Olympic Stadium, Berlin. 'Stirring Aryan followers to new heights of frenzied and evil patriotism'. (Ph Imperial War Museum)

confined spaces of street and square could not provide. The 'visible focus' was quite clearly intended to be the orator with an impressive stage-set behind him whilst the visible force was to be the assembled masses, creating what Taylor describes as a 'whole and spiritual community'.

The emphasis which Nazi propaganda laid on 'community experience' was to be seen most clearly in the large spectacles. Here, the detailed and ingenious use of technical devices induced and heightened the degree of frenzy in the crowd. Often, the event culminated in the entrance of the Führer, thus implying the role of Hitler as high priest bringing hope and glory to the community, thus extending the notion of political rally to semi-religious, quasi-magical ritual.

At Tempelhof field Speer attempted to create a visible focus 'so large and powerful that it would act as a symbol of the event, as an expression of the assembling masses of people'. This consisted of a podium 100 metres long behind which thousands of Nazi banners could be draped from a flag tribune. The rally was held at night and Speer wrote of the event: 'The mountain of flags made radiant by thousands of lights stood with its glaring red in stark contrast to the dark blue evening sky, while all irrelevant and intrusive elements sank away into the evening twilight'.[22] It was to this type of impressive backdrop that the 'visible force' of the masses would address itself. This close attention to technical detail was crucial to the success of the Nazi rally, and the nature of the event was heightened by the construction of a compelling scenario which raised political expression to the heights of religious ritual. The greatest example of this type of spectacle

occurred at Nuremberg in the Zeppelin field where, by using hundreds of upturned anti-aircraft lights spaced around the edge of the parade ground, Speer created 'mighty pillars of infinitely high outer walls'. Sir Neville Henderson, whilst stressing the theatricality of the occasion, described the effect as both solemn and beautiful.[23]

Similarly, the Berlin Olympic Stadium designed by Werner March was to do far more than serve as a focal point for the 1936 Olympic Games. Besides being a showpiece for the world to see, it was also to serve as a national centre. Sculptures by Kolbe and Breker idealised the Nordic ancestry of the 'new' German man whilst the multi-purpose fixtures of the arena made it possible to hold 'great parades, choral festivals, nationalist concerts, military and equestrian concerts and shows'. Richard D. Mandell's book, *The Nazi Olympics* concludes that Hitler used the games, the athletes and the benighted Olympic officials to stir his followers to 'new heights of frenzied and evil patriotism'.[24] On these occasions all sense of individual responsibility was removed: the apocalyptic visions of the regime were to substitute individually meaningful thoughts or actions with total self-sacrifice and participation in the comunal *volk* entity. It was this concept of the crowd, and the individual's necessary submission to it, which was the essence of National Socialism.

The Crowd

Alfred Rosenberg believed that 'race' was *the* basic concept.[25] In other words, there was no universal doctrine for all men. He stressed that the arts of Greece should serve as a basis for racial

10 Rally in Zeppelin field in Nuremberg organised by Speer. This building has many references to the Modern Movement.

expression in the German man: the production of art and architecture is an effort of the will to unburden itself, to manifest the racial personality. Individualism and universality are both alien to the national unit, the *volk*.[26] This stress upon culture as being 'truly expressive of the eternally creative essence of race' was echoed by Hitler in 1937. 'The new man must be a culturally-centred, creative person who through his creative drives activates his Germanism'. This idea was always stressed in Nazi idealogy and it can be argued that it reflected the frustration of the individual in an increasingly industrialised society.

Just as this boundary between culture and political ideology had been broken down, so too was the distinction between public and private life. To the Nazis, as to the Communists, individualism had to be abolished for it was part of the mentality which had induced friction within society itself.[27] Under the Nazis, man had found a sense of belonging based upon his membership of a glorious community.

In 1865 Gustav Le Bon wrote of the 'conservatism of crowds' which tends to cling to certain dieas. Hitler built upon this notion, writing that the success of his movement as a mass religion bore out his view that 'magical powers' were needed to control the masses. Le Bon, although writing many years earlier, was essentially questioning rational human behaviour in what he called the 'era of crowds': 'we see, then, the disappearance of the conscious personality, the predominance of the unconscious personality, the turning by means of suggestion and contagion the feelings and ideas in an identical directon: the tendency to immediately transform the suggested

ideas into acts. These we see are the principal characteristics of the individuals that form a crowd'.[28]

The Plurality of Architectural Styles

Architecturally, then, it would appear that the 'soldierly discipline' of National Socialist monumental classicism and the formal and symbolic distribution of street, avenue, and square attempted by means of scale to express the regime's aggressive ideology and war-like intentions. Despite the ideologist's declarations of Nordic synthesis in the development of German Neoclassicism, the notion of architecture as a static expression of political ideology has on many occasions been questioned.[29] It has been pointed out that Neoclassicism saw a revival in France, Italy, Britain, America and even Russia during the nineteen-thirties, all expressing different purposes or beliefs. German fascist architecture did not *speak* Nazism but rather became the symbol, through intense propaganda, of the awakening of particularly 'German' cultural values. Consistent with the contradictory nature of the Nazi movement, however, Nazi Architecture by no means simply returned to the great styles of the past. Its references to the Modern Movement, in both massing and horizontal orientation are quite clear. The Olympic Stadium, Goering's air ministry, the Chancellery, all in Berlin, and the Zeppelin field, Nuremberg, all portray explicit references to the radical style so criticised in the early nineteen-twenties.

Monumental classicism was by no means the only architectural style of the regime. The *Ordensburgen* (order castles, intended for training the elite, were built in a form of

79

11 *Ordensburgen* (order castles), a form of romanesque style expressing 'Nordic solidity and reserve'.

12 The Tannenburg Memorial, another form of romanesque imitation. 'They breathe calm and firmness, relaxation and peace in their strong thick walls': Johannes Eilemann.

13 These experimental air force buildings were often described in the Nazi journals as representing 'true practicality and crystal-clear functionalism'.

romanesque style, as were the Dahlem tower, intended for work on splitting the atom, and the Tannenburg Memorial, built to commemorate President Hindenburg. By contrast, small housing settlements (*Siedlungen*) very often utilised local vernacular traditions whilst some industrial buildings, for example the air force experimental buildings with their slim steel structures and glass and brick infill panels, could easily have been the work of the nineteen-twenties radicals.

It is clear that the regime placed a great deal of stress on the importance of art and architecture, which were used to symbolise a cultural renaissance. By skilfully exploiting and manipulating individual alienation through mass ritual, the regime attempted to bring about a 'Germanic' view, one deeply embedded in a paranoia stemming from the post-First World War years.

'I am convinced' declared Hitler, 'that art, since it forms the most uncorrupted, the most immediate reflection of peoples' souls, exercises unconsciously by far the greatest influence on the masses of the people'.[30] It is indeed ironic that, characteristic of most authoritarian regimes, it was the *Party* that created a powerful image and disguised the horrifying reality of an oppressed society. The party slogan, 'The common good before the individual good', covered walls, banners, posters and party manifestos, sending its message to an alienated people too blind to the price to be paid.

Benjamin Warner
Born 1954. Studied at Brighton Polytechnic 1973-76 (B.A.) and at Polytechnic of Central London 1978-80 (Dip. Arch.). Has worked with P.S.A. in Croydon (1976-77), 'Feniz Arguitetura' in Sao Paulo, Brazil (1977-78), Stanley Peach & Partners, London (1980-81) and is currently with Masayuki Kurokawa Associates in Tokyo.

Notes

1 Erich Fromm, *Escape from Freedom,* New York, 1965, pp234-5, as cited in *Ideology and Participation,* edited by Douglas E. Ashford, Sage Publications Inc., 1972.
2 Gustav Le Bon, *The Crowd,* London, 1922, pp35-6.
3 This may be seen as the standard explanation of the conditions operative in the evolution of fascism.
4 Adolf Hitler, *Mein Kampf,* 1943.
5 Fromm, *op. cit.*
6 Lehmann Haupt, *Art Under Dictatorship,* 1954.
7 All those who had been members of the Berlin *Novembergruppe.*
8 Lehmann Haupt, *op. cit.*
9 'Aus der Asphaltkultur', *Volkische Beobachter,* July 1928.
10 *Volkische*: a word derived from *Volk* (people, tribe or race but with mystical overtones.
11 Walter Darré: Consultant to Prussian Ministry of Agriculture in 1927 and later influential in the Nazi Party.
12 Walter Darré, *The Peasantry as the Life Source of the Nordic Race.*
13 Robert R. Taylor, *The Word in Stone,* University of California Press, 1974, pp157-181.
14 Alan Bullock, *Hitler: A Study in Tyranny,* Penguin, London.
15 Taylor, *op. cit.*
16 J.P. Weber, 'Aspects of National Socialist Architecture', *Architectural Association Quarterly,* London, p55.
17 *Domarus,* 1965, p778.
18 Albert Speer, *Inside the Third Reich,* Verlag Ullstein Gmbtt, 1969, p153.
19 *Ibid.,* pp151-160.
20 Hitler, speech to the Reichstag, 1937.
21 Weber, *op. cit.,* p.51.
22 Albert Speer, *Die Aufbauten auf dem Tempelhofer Feld in Berlin, Zum Mai 1933,* 1933.
23 Sir Neville Henderson, *Failure of a Mission,* New York, 1940.
24 Peter Axthelm, *Newsweek,* January, 1980.
25 Chandler, *Rosenberg's Nazi Myth.*
26 *Ibid.*
27 George Mosse, *Nazi Culture: Intellectual, Cultural and Social Life in the Third Reich,* W.H. Allen, 1966.
28 Le Bon, *op. cit.*
29 Gerald Bloymeyer, *International Architect,* October, 1980.
30 *Domarus,* 1965.

Wolfgang Schäche
Nazi Architecture and its Approach to Antiquity

A Criticism of the 'Neoclassical' Argument, with reference to the Berlin Museum Plans

Berlin's architectural and municipal history would appear to have been fully and adequately set forth in numerous publications. A study of these works, however, reveals that an abundance of questions – some of them quite weighty – have remained unanswered, or indeed not even raised. Particularly striking about the more recent (ie post-1945) literature on Berlin which analyses the city's architectural evolution is that the period 1933-45 has been largely ignored.[1] This discovery does not, of course, apply only to Berlin but is generally true of the whole field.

Until the late nineteen-sixties, the artistic output of National Socialism in general, and its architecture in particular, was practically excluded from German art history.[2] Academic analysis of it ran parallel to a political assimilation of the Third Reich by the West German public. Just as any inquiry as to the intrinsic character of fascism and its social determinants was suppressed by diverting the discussion onto a moralistic level, so, similarly, the visual arts of German fascism had been placed under a taboo by official art history. 'As far as Nazi architecture in Germany is concerned, even one word on the subject is excessive', Nikolaus Pevsner wrote in the standard work, *Europäische Architektur*.[3] Wherever the subject of Nazi architecture was actually touched upon, learned perceptions were limited either to descriptive statements or alternatively to comparative style-analysis, whose conclusions largely exhausted themselves in stereotypical explanations of 'non-art'. The conclusions of such investigations were the necessary consequence of a methodology which assumes that architecture is not to be conceived of as a manifestation of social conditioning, but is interpreted – in history generally and architectural history in particular – as a series of individual phenomena precipitated by definite social factors. History is thereby presented as the story of people, as a string of dated events – and, by analogy, artistry is seen as the brain-child of brilliant and not-so-brilliant men.

By the early nineteen-seventies the 'assimilation-by-suppression' approach was being significantly corrected as young critical minds in art historical research, by questioning and pondering the contents of their own field and its 'learned traditions',[4] broke through the taboo surrounding the Third Reich's art and introduced it as a subject into the 'Debate on Fascism,' now being conducted inter-disciplinarily. From then on there appeared a 'growing number of critical erudite publications on painting, architecture and town-planing under fascism, which endeavoured to analyse and evaluate such art against the background of the system of social relationships'[5] and which sought to define the determining factors.[6]

Such a development makes it all the more interesting to observe, in the context of the stylistic designation of Nazi architecture, that it is still being obstinately defined as a form of Neoclassicism. This classification – encountered in the earliest one-dimensional studies of style – relates to the so-called official architecture of State and Party buildings, and ignores the architecture employed in industry, the highways, private dwellings, and housing estates. Along with research that is dominated by this attitude, it is also uncritically adopted by some of the post-1970 studies which regard themselves as surveys in social criticism – even though the concomitant statements and conclusions on the analysis of fascist architecture display an inherently different quality.[7] Despite the considerable differences in methodology, the argument always proceeds via the same examples. The Munich buildings erected back in 1933 by Paul Ludwig Troost, 'the Führer's first master-builder', are treated as the definitive architecture of National Socialism.[8] The Nuremberg edifices for the Party's conference campus ('Reichsparteitagsgelände') – notably the tribune on the Zeppelin Field – are cited as the continuation of this. Finally, the New Reich Chancellery (1938-9) in Berlin, by Albert Speer, is worked up as the 'key creation of the Nazi regime'[9] – an edifice with 'a powerful Neoclassical facade'.[10] This purports adequately to define Nazi architecture as 'the Neoclassicism of Troost and Speer'.[11] To this Neoclassicism is ascribed a 'specific hardness',[12] and its model is 'German classicism (especially Schinkel), whose orientation again and again – in detail, plan and elevation, as well as in town-planning generally – refers back to this epoch'.[13] Adolf Hitler's architectonic aspirations on the one hand[14] and, on the other, the Nazi ideology that is attributed to him and to Alfred Rosenberg, are adduced as the determining motives for the adoption of such a style: 'Through Nazi ideology, as established by Rosenberg and translated into radical reality by Hitler, architecture in Germany became regimented into a Neoclassical tradition'.[15]

This raises the question whether Nazi architecture as limited to State and Party buildings[16] may truly be described as Neoclassical and how far – if at all – such a stylistic classification is capable of shedding light on inter-relationships and of facilitating insights which explain this architecture in terms of its specific role within National Socialism. Even if this term were actually to prove relevant in this way, the question remains as to how the level of perception justifying it as a concept is conditioned. This means examining Nazi architecture with a view to establishing whether its supposed adoption of antique styles of architecture refers to their inherent qualities or merely to the forms that were taken up – or again, whether Nazi architecture relates directly to antiquity or appears as an adaptation of classicism. If one then embarks upon the Neoclassical theory and pursues it, then, in accordance with the universal claim that it fully explains Nazi architecture, it is bound to be verifiable against a tangible example. Hence it must apply to all the 'Party and State buildings', ie not only to the few show-pieces that were actually carried out, such as Troost's and Speer's edifices mentioned above: it must also apply *par excellence* to the many projects that were prepared everywhere in line with the so-called 'Reformation Measures'. In quantitative terms, too, these ultimately represent Nazi architecture.

The Berlin 'Reformation Plans', which commenced in 1937 following Speer's appointment as chief building inspector (GBI) to the Reich capital, offer the most obvious subjects for

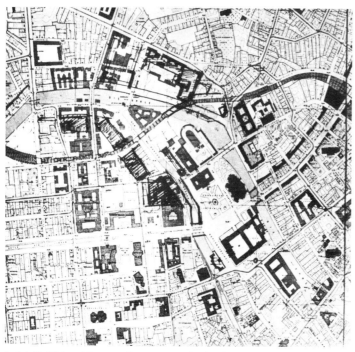

1 Adolf Hitler, Museum Quarter: rough sketch on ordnance survey map c 1934.

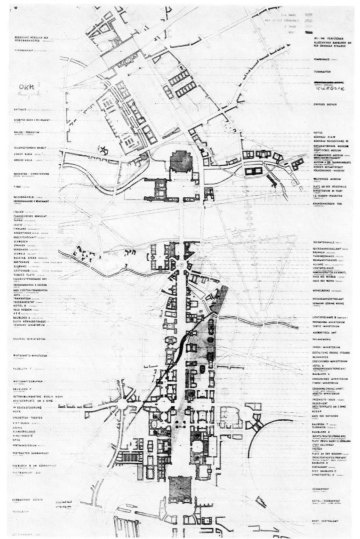

2 GBI, plan of the Museum Quarter: drawing (extract from ordnance survey map, north-south axis), final planning stage, late 1942.

scrutiny. These announce themselves through the absolute priority which Berlin indisputedly had in the Third Reich's official development programme. Out of the political requirement that the Reich capital, too, should manifest in specifically architectural form the Nazi claim to supremacy, there evolved a city plan which both in its architectonic proportions and in the associated financial outlay smashed every comparable scale of things. In accordance with the intended 'Claim to Eternity' the buildings and projects had an exemplary function which would determine the aesthetic of plans for other 'Reformation Cities'.[17]

The 'Reformation Plans' – which cannot here be enlarged upon – included a project for a new museum quarter to adjoin the old Museum Island ('Museumsinsel'), but exceeding the latter's surface area several times over – a major building complex which claimed particular attention. Its execution would have constituted the greatest intervention in the physical structure of an inner city, which in itself makes it an interesting example. Its proximity to the historic centre and the presence, close at hand, of the buildings of 'Prusso-Spartan classicism' shows a study of these projects' style and aesthetic vocabulary to be all the more significant. Lars Olof Larsson, the latest protagonist of the 'Neoclassical' argument in his book *Die Neugestaltung der Reichshauptstadt*,[18] wrote – with downright unconcerned naivety – 'the new museums were to have been the Third Reich's tribute to the Berlin of Schinkel's and Schlüter's day, and they were to bear comparison with the buildings generally regarded as the most important in Berlin: Palace, Zeughaus, and the museums by Schinkel and Stüler. This demanded much of the architects entrusted with these tasks.'[19] And of the museums' architects, Wilhelm Kreis and Hans Dustmann, he wrote, 'The choice of Wilhelm Kreis should come to us here as no surprise. He was at that time one of the leading figures among German architects, and his artistic abilities were highly prized in the Third Reich... Dustmann...was one of the architects to whom |Speer| readily gave monumental commissions.'[20]

The planned extension of Museum Island, which in 1930 was resolved to develop, along with Alfred Messel's Pergamon Museum,[21] was being discussed between Hitler and the Municipal Planning Office as early as 1934. Afterwards it was initially arranged that 'the river-banks to the east and west of |Museum Island|' should be developed by building 'a Germanic Museum, an Applied Arts Museum' and 'new accommodation for the Egyptian Department and...Asiatic art'.[22] A sketch submitted by Hitler showing the individual building units on the current site-plan illustrates this idea –which was not immediately worked up as a plan, however.[23] It was only in the context of the 'Reformation Plans', mentioned above, that the idea was taken up again, after 1937, and made tangible. By the time that all planning for the museums was suspended (1943), the following conception was established: north of the River Spree, between Friedrichstrasse in the west and Stadtsbahnstrasse in the east, a set of 'three interrelated museum edifices' was to arise, following 'in plan the long curve of the Spree'.[24] The western building on the Friedrichstrasse was designed for the Eastern Asiatic Museum,[25] the central complex for the Egyptian Museum and the eastern construction for the Germanic Museum. To the south of the railway embankment a museum restaurant and the Museum of the Nineteenth Century were added. Along the southern bank of the Spree, opposite the Eastern Asiatic and Egyptian Museums, was sited the elongated shape of the Ethnological Museum.[26] South-east of the railway embankment, along the Kupfergraben, stood the World War Museum, which as an extension of the Zeughaus

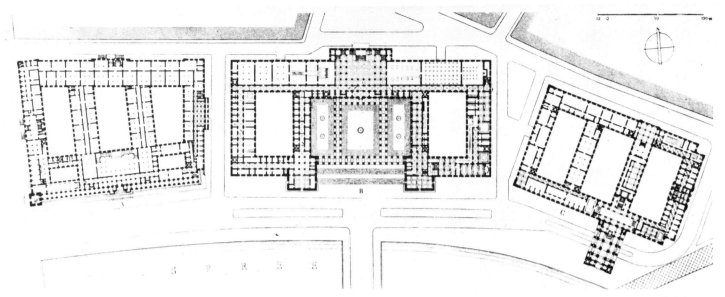

3 W. Kreis, Museum Quarter: plan of the respective first floors of the Museum of the Nineteenth Century (later Eastern Asiatic Museum), the Egyptian Museum and the Germanic Museum, drawing, planning stage, 1940-1.

was designed to be connected to it via a 'corridor area'.[27] A second portion of the building on Hegelplatz, facing the northern frontage of the University, was linked – again by a 'corridor area' – from the rear facade of the building to the west, to the elongated building on the Kupfergraben. The construction of a new Applied Arts Museum (under consideration in 1934) no longer formed any part of the programme by now. Some of the designs of the Eastern Asiatic, Egyptian and Germanic Museums, together with those of the World War Museum and Ethnological Museum became ready for execution. On the other hand, planning for the Museum of the Nineteenth Century and the central museum restaurant did not get beyond the preliminary design phase. These two projects have yielded only illustrations of the block models.

In the Ethnological Museum the exhibits of the old house on Prinz-Albrecht-Strasse were to be united with those from the 1916 building in Berlin-Dahlem, while in the Eastern Asiatic and Egyptian Museums the collections from Messel's Pergamon Museum were to be housed,[28] and the World War Museum was envisaged for the arms and military equipment of the First and Second World Wars. By contrast, neither was the conception of the Museum of the Nineteenth Century firmly established nor had definitive ideas evolved as to what objects

the Germanic Museum should house.[29]

The buildings to be sacrificed in constructing the Eastern Asiatic, Egyptian and Germanic Museums on the northern bank, designed by Wilhelm Kreis, included the University clinic, plus Monbijou Palace and its park. The World War Museum, also planned by Kreis, would have displaced the entire historic development along the Kupfergraben (notably dwellings from the eighteenth and early nineteenth centuries), while Dustmann's Ethnology Museum would have done away with the Admiral's Palace which in those days stood on Friedrichstrasse (today the Metropoltheater). Lastly, for both the Museum of the Nineteenth Century and the central museum restaurant created by the architectural partnership of Dammeier and Ulrich, a large apartment block in the district between Spandauer Strasse and Neue Friedrichstrasse (now Littenstrasse) was due to be demolished. This would totally have changed the face of this traditional inner city area.

Turning to the architecture of the projected museums which henceforth were to replace the organic building texture and to characterise the Spree's banks between Friedrichstrasse Station and the pleasure gardens, one observes of the buildings that, although they would in their vertical dimensions have largely fitted into the existing development, their volume and surface

4 W. Kreis, Museum Quarter, northern bank of the Spree: view of the Museum of the Nineteenth Century (later Eastern Asiatic Museum), the Egyptian Museum and the Germanic Museum, pen-and-ink drawing, 1940-1.

5 GBI, Museum Quarter, general view: in the left foreground the Ethnological Museum by H. Dustmann. Architect's model, planning stage in 1940-1.

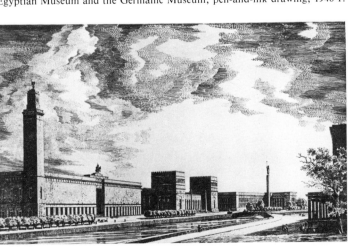

areas unmistakably display the 'new' quality which found its most gross expression in the constructions for the north-south axis – the projected 'Street of Splendour of the Reich capital'.[31] The site area of the Ethnological Museum alone (approximately 275 x 110 m) – the largest of the proposed buildings –would have equalled the entire developed area on Museum Island. The enormous surface-area, the vast volume that went with it, and its exposed position all serve to make it the most forceful complex within the scheme. Its visual dominance is further emphasised by mounting its massively heavy bulk on a stepped plinth. The building proper is composed of three sections. A tall central unit, arranged crosswise, connects two flatter enclosed blocks, each of which forms an inner courtyard. Around the ground floor there 'runs a projecting arcade in Doric order'.[32] The first-floor windows, together with the frieze, cornice and attic storey subdivide the ashlar-dressed masonry forming the facade. However, where Larsson claims to discern formal ties with the New Museum by Stüler,[33] a hollow rhetoric and brutalised bulk underlie the structure. The building's hard abrupt angularity, the dismissive and enclosed character evoked by the absence of second-floor windows and accentuated by the fortress-like stratification of the portal's frontage, speak a language of shrill fortification and menacing inaccessibility. Although structurally antique elements are incorporated (Doric columns, triglyphic frieze, etc.), these are distorted by scale and proportion until they become unrecognisable. In the central section the triglyphs turn into individual or joined fluted pilasters; the inserted uprights with their stylised Corinthian capitals would have been indiscernible as such to anyone entering, and would be seen only as a harsh mass of stone. Its inhuman outsize scale demotes the 'Doric columns' of the arcades to the rank of puny architectural pawns which can only make any impact when strung together. For the sake of a predominant monumentality, deriving from sheer bulk and volume, and aiming in effect to discipline and intimidate, the structure has been brutally coarsened and the individuality of detail thereby nullified. The 'monolithic mass transmits an aura of immutability'[34] designed to force the individual into line with the arrayed masses. This would have been the only way of entering into a viable relationship with this architecture. The suppression of the lone architectural feature complemented the social suppression of the individual. Dustmann's Ethnology Museum articulated no true antique language of forms, nor did its aesthetic vocabulary convey any qualitative relationship with the buildings of the classical period. Comparing even the Kaiser-Friedrich-Museum (now the Bode Museum) standing on the north-western tip of Museum Island and constructed between 1898 and 1903 by Ernst von Ihne, 'a typical advocate of lofty *wilhelminisch* Baroque'[35] – even this appeared reticent, simple and well-proportioned when set against the Ethnological Museum.

The elongated form of the World War Museum, intended to fit on the Kupfergraben opposite the Pergamon Museum and the New Museum, is more varied than the Ethnology Museum, both in its formal repertoire and in the proportions of the individual building segments. In scale it takes its bearings from Schlüter's Zeughaus. The respective floors are equal in height. Again, the differentiation of the storeys recurs: the Zeughaus has an ashlar-faced ground floor and a rough-cast upper floor, while the World War Museum has a highly rusticated ground floor and an upper floor that is variously ashlar-faced and colonnaded. The attempt to relate the building with the Zeughaus on the one hand and with the Pergamon and New Museums on the other has visibly overtaxed the planner. He was in any case

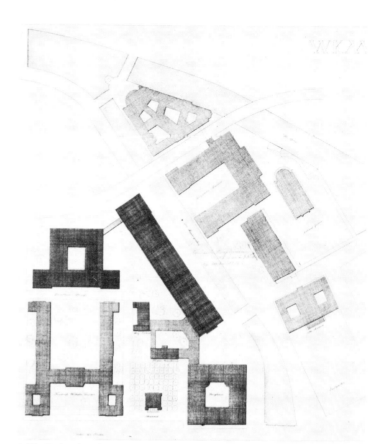

6 W. Kreis, site plan of the World War Museum (below right the old Zeughaus): drawing, planning stage, 1941-2.

7 W. Kreis, World War Museum: view of the long structure on the Kupfergraben (first building phase), architect's model, planning stage 1941.

8 W. Kreis, World War Museum: projected link with the old Zeughaus, pen-and-ink drawing, 1941.

9 H. Dustmann, Ethnological Museum: general view, architect's model, planning stage, 1941-2.

10 GBI, Museum Quarter view along the Spree towards the Kaiser-Friedrich-Museum (now the Bode-Museum), to the right the Ethnological Museum, architect's model, planning stage, 1941-2.

unable to escape his own past and imagined the solution to lie in the architecture of his 'Bismarck towers and national monuments' which are strongly evoked here.[36] The Museum's defensive quality – which also governed Dustmann's designs –matched the characer of such memorials. The slope of the rusticated facade, the hatch-like window embrasures on the ground floor, the closed and stony facings to the end-sections together with the dense colonnade on the long central section –all contributed to the militancy of this architecture. The cannon, mounted on high pedestals at each of the four roof-corners of the two end-sections, serve to heighten its fortress-like character. Its forbidding aspect was supposed to reflect the function of the museum, a symbolism attributable to the outgoing nineteenth century and not encountered even in modified form either in antiquity or in classicism. It may thus be observed that the World War Museum, to a greater extent than the Ethnological Museum, adopted pseudo-classical styles, albeit with simplifications (eg in the cornice design and colonnade), and pressed architecture into service as a message-bearer, thereby linking it indirectly to the monumental architecture of the early twentieth century.

The Eastern Asiatic Museum, destined for the northern bank of the Spree, is formally related to the Ethnological Museum: its sparse ornamentation is reduced even more radically to plain geometric shapes, and echoes the fortress-like character of the other two buildings by virtue of its blind front facade, relieved only by an arcade punctuated by plain, joined pillars. The tower on the eastern corner underlines this militancy and also lends the facade imperious overtones. In the context of this building Larsson obliquely confesses that here (as well) the 'Neoclassical' argument proves to be inappropriate: he writes, 'The obvious models for this construction may well be Adolf Abel's exhibition hall for the 1927-8 press exhibition in Cologne and, above all, Ragnar Östberg's town hall in Stockholm

of 1923. Yet it...evidently ties up with Kreis' own work as well. It may be compared with the exhibition buildings for the Gesolei Exhibition in Düsseldorf.'[37]

On the Egyptian Museum, however, one discerns 'block-like bastions, which in design and material are reminiscent of the heyday of Ancient Assyrian municipal architecture'.[38] The stylised incorporation of Assyrian motifs and ornaments (especially in the relief friezes on the towers) is overlaid by the 'pseudo-Egyptian designs'[39] of the entrance colonnade and by the erection of two obelisks in front of the main steps. Here,too, there are quasi-historical allusions to the styles of widely differing eras and cultures, producing architecture that cannot be classified as Neoclassical.

Lastly, in the case of the Germanic Museum it would have been particularly apposite to observe Nazi racial theories according to which 'Nordic men... created... Greek civilization' and 'the finest dream of Nordic man was dreamt in Hellas',[40] by building along antique lines in order to display visually the cultural claims being vehemently advanced, and as an expression of the 'innate feeling that Germanic and Greek culture grew from the self-same root.'[41] Kreis' design appears as an enclosed block of approximately 180 x 100 m, with transversal divisions separating the interior into three courtyards. A lateral projection in the nature of a portico, screening Uferstrasse from the urban railway, forms the visual back-drop to a tall fluted pillar surmounted by a sculpture whose appearance and attributes suggest Athena.[43] The facades, sharply segmented, are symmetrical. A massive sloping base of rusticated stone, raised at the corners right up to the cornice, frames the facade areas formed by two upper storeys. The first floor is characterised by tall windows set into smooth, broad jambs, but without sills. This means that they abut hard onto the rustication, whose rough-hewn stonework is broken only by small openings. Between the window-jambs the pillars of the visually

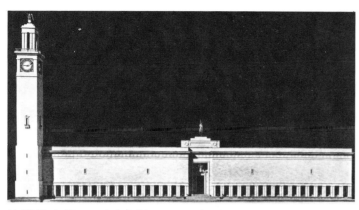

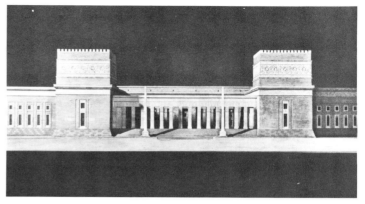

11 W. Kreis, Eastern Asiatic Museum (previously the proposed Museum of the Nineteenth Century): general view, architect's model, planning stage, 1942.

12 W. Kreis, Egyptian Museum: general view, architect's model, planning stage, 1942.

dominant second floor are repeated in the form of pilasters. The angular colonnades of the second floor, with corridors running behind them, join the entablature to form a stark framework upon which rests the cornice. On top of this there stands a tall, unadorned attic representing a further storey, but one which communicates with the exterior only through tiny vertical spy-slits. The structure of the facade extends into the portico straddling the street, whose colonnade reaches up through all the floors. Two of its five apertures are for motor traffic, the rest being reserved for passers-by and visitors. Set above the great front steps is the Museum's main entrance. On the four slightly raised corners of the portico, fire-bowls directly related to some unidentifiable Attic ornament are arranged. The eye-catching feature of the whole layout is the pillar first mentioned above, which rises from a stepped base and is crowned by a figure erected on a plinth above the cornice.

The ideological preconceptions as to the building's purpose dictated its architectonic form. The erection of Athena is the most obvious expression of this. The portico may similarly be perceived as the association of antique city gateways and triumphal arches. Only through such prominent symbolical allusions can the basic claim to the authorship of ancient Greek culture[44] be proclaimed. The formal line of argument does not restrict itself to the original quotation but launches out into an unfettered interpretation. This means that the aesthetic plane of reference alone is not conclusive. Neither antique architecture itself nor its adoption by the classical movement is the determining factor, but only 'the possibilities it offers for monumental design'.[45] The Germanic Museum's configuration illustrates this: it, too, features reduced shapes (in the supports, capitals and cornice), an emphatic massiveness (heavy, bulky rustication) and a defiant bastion-architecture (portico design, corner towers, and attic storey). The object was to safeguard and defend the Nazi idea of Germanic civilisation down through the perspective of 'a thousand years'. Architecture had to create the appropriate framework for this, and to act as message-bearer.

In conclusion, it seems clear that the 'Neoclassical' argument, when measured against the plans for the new Berlin Museum Quarter (displayed here as being representative of the 'Berlin Reformation Measures' generally), proves to be inappropriate in getting at the fundamentals of Nazi architecture in terms of its stylistic repertoire. Firstly, it cannot be described as Neoclassical in the narrower sense of 'classicism' meaning, historically, 'the rationalistic counter-movement... to... Baroque'[46] and based upon 'simplicity and proportion'[47], severity and discipline as exemplified by Graeco-Roman

models.[48] Secondly, the enlarged concept of Neoclassicism – as 'aid to communication'[49] – proposed by K. Arndt fails to afford an adequate basis for defining the nature of Nazi architecture: indeed, its very originators rejected such an association. 'Anyone looking at our great public edifices who refers to "Neoclassicism" has failed to understand the essence of our mode of building. This essence lies in the new task ahead, in the new all-embracing purpose in our constructions which are unprecedented in their ground-plan, spatial layout and integrated shape, and which derive exclusively from the spirit of our National Socialist life.'[50] 'The buildings of the movement are heroic, which accords with their very essence. Putting up any and every utilitarian building... along these lines would be wrong and spurious. Precisely this requirement also shows that the Reich's architecture is not a stylistic imitation of classicism (as in the nineteenth century, say) which tries to apply universally one fashionable design'.[51] And this 'heroic architecture', where 'the criterion of the individual... gives way... to that of the military unit' and whose 'organic formation... reflects the disciplined marching of the columns'[52] takes up aesthetic models wherever they seem likely to suggest 'grandeur and monumentality'. This is clarified further when Georg Schorer discerns in Speer's Reich Chancellery 'that mature style on the European scale which, trained by the great styles of History and yet close to the present, is a clear expression of the broad cultural aspiration of our modern times and of its embodiment in the Occident's heritage'.[54]

Hence classical architecture was only one level of perception within the framework of an historicising adaptation of an aesthetic repertoire consisting of the design resources from the entirety of Western architecture. The much-cited connection with Prussian classicism[55] served National Socialism rather as a means of verbally justifying its own building projects than as an architectonic paradigm. Its purpose was to legitimize. Wherever classical elements actually were used, the grotesque exaggeration of their proportions forced them into a monumentality whose 'effect was more akin to Egyptian tyranny than Hellenic humanism'.[56] Its colossal excesses do indeed embody a certain inner consistency ('Eigengesetzlichkeit') such as J. Petsch concedes to Nazi architecture. Its fortified, memorial and sepulchral features 'pursue the objective |of| stimulating mental associations and of expounding the heroic character of the Nazi *Weltanschauung:* the emotive allusions are used to imbue people with Nazi ideology'.[57]

Thus J. Kunst describes it logically as 'architectura militans', whose task was 'to exhibit power and force at the bidding of its builders'.[58] The 'rectilinearity', 'clarity' and 'severity' which typify it have, however, ceased to be the concepts relating to

13 W. Kreis, Germanic Museum eastern view, architect's model, planning stage, 1941.

14 W. Kreis, Germanic Museum front view, model, planning stage, 1941.

classicism. Through their megalomaniacal scale they take on a new dimension. Having escaped from all human proportions, this architecture arrays its columns and squares to suggest massed human ranks. The fortified and sepulchral character of the structures serves to militarise these masses and to prepare them for war and death.[59] Seen in this perspective, this 'National Socialist style', so reflective of its inner purpose, may be regarded (if at all) as a 'monumentalism' – following on formally and thematically from the 'architecture of *Wilhelminisch* Germany', which allows it to be viewed 'as the "organic development of the original approach" adopted by imperial building in about 1910'[60] Besides the deeper affinity – for in both cases the architectural styles were being formulated on the eve of imperial wars – the connection was further emphasised by the personal continuity of the architects. The employment of Troost, Kreis, Bestelmeyer, Bonatz and Behrens during the Third Reich era exemplified this.

The term 'Neoclassical', although applicable to a few buildings, is not for general use, and in defining Nazi architecture –whether by reference to its intrinsic or its formal character, and even when narrowing it down to 'Party and State buildings' – it is inappropriate and technically confusing. This is bound to be so, since the methodology linked with the argument ignores vital factors in architecture which derive from economic conditions. But if we are to explain the major importance of Nazi building activity in its social context, its specific economic status must be defined. Only the resultant conclusions make it possible to elucidate the political and aesthetic function assigned to building work in the complicated web and the utilisation mechanisms conditioning it.[61] 'The size of the individual structures and the scope of the total building programme, and its fundamental role in the economy as a whole forbid us to see it almost exclusively in terms of its functions which are largely apparent only on the exterior. Not until the primary (ie economic) functions of fascist building have been analysed is it meaningful to enquire into its style and its propaganda functions.'[62] The development of architecture in the first half of the twentieth century followed the social developments which moved from the time of the Kaiser through the Weimar Republic into fascism. Of architecture in the years 1933-45, if explicitly explored for its attitude towards antiquity, we can say that only an oblique but not a direct connection with antiquity or classicism is discernible, which is expressed by the adoption, at one remove, of the monumental architecture of the Kaiser's day, but which confines itself to form alone.

Translated from the German by Robin Charleston

Wolfgang Schäche
Born in Berlin 1948. Studied architecture at the Technische Universität Berlin and qualified as 'Diplom-Ingenieur' in 1972. Since that time has worked as a historian of architecture and is specialised in the history of architecture and town-development of the nineteenth and twentieth centuries. From 1975-77 was private assistant to Professor Dr h.c. Julius Posener. Since 1977 has been working at the Institut für Architektur-und Stadtgeschichte of the Technische Universität Berlin both in research and teaching. His special centres of research are the architecture and town development of Berlin and the architecture of fascism. Has published a number of works on these subjects.

Notes

1 This applies equally to the other art forms: see J. Petsch's *Baukunst und Stadtplanung im Dritten Reich*, 1976, p 9.
2 The few exceptions which did deal with this subject come from other areas of study: H. Brenner, *Die Kunstpolitik des Nationalsozialismus*, 1963; J. Wulf, *Die Bildenden Künste im Dritten Reich*, 1963; A. Teut, *Architektur im Dritten Reich*, 1967.
3 N. Pevsner, *Europäische Architektur'* 2nd ed 1967, p 466.
4 cf. also: M. Warnke (ed.), *Das Kunstwerk zwischen Wissenschaft und Weltanschauung*, 1970.
5 J. Petsch, 'Wiederkehr Nationalsozialistischer Kunst', published in the *Frankfurter Rundschau* of 28 August 1978, p 14.
6 Of special note here are the exhibition and its catalogue *Kunst im 3.Reich, Dokumente der Unterwerfung*, 1974, presented by the Frankfurt Art Circle in conjunction with a working group from Frankfurt University's Art Historical Institute; and B. Hinz, *Die Malerei im Deutschen Faschismus*, 1974. These were followed by (among others) K. Herding, H. Mittig, *Kunst und Alltag im NS-System, Albert Speers Berliner Strassenlaternen*, 1975 and by Petsch, *op. cit.*
7 For example, we find that the catalogue of the Frankfurt Exhibition (note 6, p 50) uses the concept of Neoclassicism, albeit by way of a quotation referring to the classification of 'Party and State buildings'.
8 That is, the 'Führer's Building', the 'Administrative Building', and the two 'Temples of Glory' on the Königsplatz. See K. Arndt/H. Döhl, *Das Wort aus Stein*, in *Publikationen zu wissenschaftlichen Filmen 1*, 1968, pp 171 ff.
9 U. Kultermann, *Die Architektur im 20. Jahrhundert*, Volume III, 1977. Contrast A. Schönberger, *Die Neue Reichskanzlei in Berlin von Albert Speer. Zum Zusammenhang von nationalsozialistischer Ideologie und Architektur*, Dissertation, FU Berlin 1978.
10 *Ibid.*
11 R. Müller-Mehlis, *Die Kunst im Dritten Reich*, 1976, p 68; Kultermann, *op. cit.*, pp 104-11.
12 Arndt, *op. cit.*, p 177.
13 *Ibid.*
14 Hitler is in this connection always endowed with an enthusiasm for antiquity. However, Speer recorded that his 'architectural world' consisted of the Paris Opera House, the buildings on Vienna's Ringstrasse and the 'pompous neobaroque' of Wilhelm II. A. Speer, *Memoirs*, 1969, pp 54 ff.
15 Kultermann, *op. cit.*, p 107.
16 Here it strikes me as dubious to submit to such limitations since they obscure the perspective on the essentials, which can only be perceived through the whole gamut of architecture.
17 W. Schäche, *Tagungsprogramm Faschismus-Kunst und visuelle Medien*, 1977, p 8.
18 L.O. Larsson, *Die Neugestaltung der Reichshauptstadt. Albert Speers Generalbebauungsplan für Berlin*, 1978.
19 *Ibid.*, p 68.
20 *Ibid.*, p 69.

21 H. Reuther, *Die Museumsinsel in Berlin*, 1978, p 38 ff.
22 J. Dülffer, J. Thies, J. Henke, *Hitlers Städte. Baupolitik im Dritten Reich*, 1978, p 98.
23 The last planning stage in the Municipal Planning Office is recorded by a plan dated 1937 (R. Wolters, *Stadtmitte Berlin*, 1978, p 131.
24 Reuther, *op. cit.*, p 40.
25 The final draft of the plan in late 1942 (see illustration 2) shows that the building originally planned as the Museum of the Nineteenth Century – west of the Egyptian Museum – is designated as the Eastern Asiatic Museum, while to the south of the projected course of the urban railway (S-Bahn) a further building is introduced as the new Museum of the Nineteenth Century. To this extent, both Larsson's (pp 65-9) and Reuther's findings are based on earlier drafts and fail to reflect the final planning stage.
26 This relates to an earlier planning stage, in about 1940-1 (see note 25).
27 Reuther, *op. cit.*, p 40.
28 The altar at Pergamon together with the processional street at Babylon were intended to be transferred to the Egyptian Museum: see Reuther, *op. cit.*, p 40.
29 Larsson, *op. cit.*, p 66. The scale of the buildings makes one suspect that copious wartime booty was being speculated upon.
30 Consideration was also given to reconstructing Monbijou Palace in the park at Charlottenburg.
31 See Speer, note 14, especially Chapter 10 (Entfesseltes Empire); also Larsson, *op. cit.*, p 38.
32 Larsson, *op. cit.*, p 68.
33 *Ibid.*
34 J. Kunst, 'Architektur und Macht. Überlegungen zur NS-Architektur in *Philipps Universität Marburg; Gazette, Comments and Reports* September 3, 1971, p 51.
35 Reuther, *op. cit.*, p 37.
36 See H. Stephan, *Wilhelm Kreis*, 1943.
37 Larsson, *op. cit.*, p 67.
38 Reuther, *op. cit.*, p 40.
39 Larsson, *op cit.*, p 67.
40 G. Schorer, *Deutsche Kunstbetrachtung*, 3rd ed 1941, p 14.
41 Stephan, *op. cit.*, p 16.
42 Neither a ground-plan nor a model of the final version has survived. It differs from the first draft in that the eastern facade forms an acute angle, with one side running parallel to the urban railway and the interior comprising only two courtyards. The intermediate version diverges from the earlier one in omitting the entrance from the eastern area (for Museum administration) mentioned above. In all the design variants, however, the facade stays the same.
43 The lance, shield, cuirass and helmet bear out this interpretation.
44 Schorer, *op. cit.*, p 14.
45 A. Speer, *Spandauer Tagebücher*, 1975, p 166.
46 Wasmuth, *Lexikon der Baukunst*, 3rd ed, 1931, p 373.
47 O. Hederer, *Klassizismus*, 1976, p 7.
48 Wasmuth, *op. cit.*, p 373.
49 K. Arndt, 'Neoklassizistische Architektur im 20. Jahrhundert' published in the *Neue Züricher Zeitung*, 22 November 1970, p 51.
50 R. Wolters, *Vom Beruf des Baumeisters*, 1944, p 46.
51 Schorer, *op. cit.*, p 150.
52 N. Stephan, *Die Baukunst im Dritten Reich*, 1939, p 10.
53 F. Tamms, 'Das Grosse in der Baukunst' in *KDR*, Issue B8, 1944, p 547.
54 Schorer, *op. cit.*, p 160.
55 See A. Speer (ed.), *Neue Deutsche Baukunst*, 4th ed, 1943, p 7.
56 Kunst, *op. cit.*, p 51. He uses this comparison with reference to the German Embassy in St Petersburg by P. Behrens, which he presents as the precursor of Nazi architecture.
57 Petsch, *op. cit.*, p 208.
58 Kunst, *op. cit.*, p 52.
59 *Ibid.*
60 Petsch, *op. cit.*, p 218.
61 Cf. W. Schäche, *op. cit.*, p 8.
62 Hinz, *op. cit.*, pp 122-9.